110649386

BUYING A BUSINESS

A GUIDE TO THE DECISIONS

Second Edition

Mike Allen and Robert Hodgkinson

ARTHUR
ANDERSEN
&CO

Graham & Trotman

A member of the Kluwer Academic Publishers Group

First published in 1986
Second edition published in 1989 by
Graham & Trotman Limited
Sterling House
66 Wilton Road
London SW1V 1DE
UK

Graham & Trotman Inc.
101 Philip Drive
Assinippi Park
Norwell, MA 02061
USA

© Arthur Andersen & Co., 1986, 1989
ISBN 1 85333 277 1

British Library Cataloguing in Publication Data
Allen, Mike, *1947–*
    Buying a business: a guide to the decisions.
    1. Great Britain. Business firms. Purchase
    I. Title   II. Hodgkinson, Robert
    658.1'6

ISBN 1–85333–277–1

Library of Congress Cataloging-in-Publication Data
Allen, Mike, 1947–
    Buying a business: a guide to the decisions/Mike Allen and
Robert Hodgkinson. —— 2nd ed.
    p. cm
    ISBN 1-85333-277-1
    1. Business enterprises–Purchasing.   I. Hodgkinson, Robert,
    1959- .   II. Title.
HD2741.A57   1989
658.1'6— dc20

89-7518
CIP

This publication is protected by international Copyright Law. All rights
reserved. No part of this publication may be reproduced, stored in a
retrieval system, or transmitted in any form or by any means, electronic,
mechanical, photocopying, recording or otherwise, without the prior
permission of the copyright holders.

Typeset in Garamond by Tradespools Ltd, Frome, Somerset
Printed and bound in Great Britain by Billing & Sons Ltd, Worcester

CONTENTS

FOREWORD
TO THE SECOND EDITION

We are indebted to all those who have helped us in writing this book, now in its second edition. Thanks are due to Dan Mace of Lovell White Durrant, Jeremy Prescott and Simon Clayton of Samuel Montagu & Co Limited and Donald Hay, Fellow of Jesus College, Oxford, who have contributed their time and talent in guiding us on the legal, commercial and economic issues connected with buying a business.

We are also deeply grateful to all the people who have given us their advice and support, including colleagues at Arthur Andersen & Co who have reviewed and typed the text and all those who have commented on the first edition.

The book is correct to the best of our knowledge and belief at the time of going to press and reflects laws, regulations and practices in force in April 1989. The views expressed are our own and are not necessarily shared by Arthur Andersen & Co.

Because the book is written as a general guide to buying a business, we recommend that specific professional advice is sought throughout the acquisition process before taking any action.

Mike Allen and Robert Hodgkinson
Arthur Andersen & Co
Manchester

April 1989

PREFACE

Since the first edition of this book was published we have witnessed great takeover scandals and the Stock Market Crash. Through it all, the pace and scale of acquisition activity has continued. The Crash has meant that some public companies no longer have highly priced shares to pay for acquisitions. On the other hand, there are private businesses which have seen their flotation hopes dashed and are only too willing to be acquired. Certain quoted companies are also seen as good acquisition targets at their post-Crash values.

Nevertheless, merger and acquisition bubbles can burst like any other bubbles and the Crash serves as a reminder that a frothy market can suddenly go flat. It might happen because of a gradual fall in profitability, confidence or the availability of funds. The apparent but continuing failure of so many deals to live up to expectations could have a similar effect. Up to now, past disappointments have perhaps stimulated the market, as the businesses involved are put up for sale again or are bought by management. In the future however, scepticism and perhaps regulation could stifle all but the best-conceived deals. For these reasons, the book continues to concentrate on quality decision-making, not the stories behind the headlines.

Our own thoughts have nonetheless evolved and therefore this second edition does not just reflect changes in regulation and legislation. We have altered the emphasis and organisation of much of the material. For example, there is a new valuation model. We give more consideration to both "leveraging", which has turned even the largest businesses into potential targets, and the "earn-out", which has made the acquisition of service businesses more attractive. We have also made the book directly relevant to management buy-out and buy-in teams and we believe that corporate buyers too will benefit from seeing how things look to such potential rivals.

Managers will, in the main, want to read about buying a business so that they feel better able to keep in view all the areas of expertise and experience that are involved. Our book aims to assist them in this and for that reason it should also be useful to sellers of businesses, professional advisers and commentators.

"Buying a Business" examines the major issues which have to be faced during the acquisition process. These issues give rise to important choices and call for informed decisions which are not made much easier by technical works of reference or catalogues of simplistic tips. Our book, in contrast, should help people buying businesses to understand the opportunities and the dangers and to manage a team which can produce solutions.

To reinforce our aim that the book should be a real "guide to the decisions" for managers, we have developed a new appendix which is a guide for managing the issues that arise during the acquisition process. We have also included a new chapter which deals with acquiring abroad. As the recent publication of a Dutch version of our book shows, the international aspects of acquisition are sure to become an increasingly important theme as physical, technical and fiscal barriers to trade are dismantled within the EEC. This is already encouraging acquisitions as businesses seek both to establish a secure base in Europe and to achieve new economies of scale within the emerging single market.

1.

SYNOPSIS

1.1 A FOUR STAGE PROCESS

There are four stages to the acquisition process.

Strategy, the first stage, is about defining the purpose that acquisition will help to realise: it answers the question, "Why?"

Search, the second stage, is about finding a feasible deal: it answers the questions, "What, where and when?"

Buying, the third stage, is about managing the buying process: it answers the questions, "How and how much?"

The aftermath, the fourth stage, is about fulfilling the strategic purpose of an acquisition: it answers the question, "So what?"

Realistic expectations of what buyers can achieve in the fourth stage after an acquisition should dominate the decision-making in the first three stages. It becomes progressively more demanding to recover from flawed decisions and management should bear in mind that the right decision at any time might be to abort an acquisition, even if significant costs have already been incurred.

Over the next four sections of this chapter, we outline our presentation of the four stages of buying a business in the chapters that follow. Although the chapters are intended to be read in sequence, they are sufficiently self-contained to allow readers to refer to individual chapters as they see fit. In Appendix I, we summarise key issues relevant at each stage of the acquisiton process and means of resolving them.

1.2 THE STRATEGIC PURPOSE

Managers need strategies to help them achieve specific business objectives in seven key areas of performance.

1. Profitability
2. Growth
3. Risk control
4. Liquidity
5. Dividends
6. Corporate image
7. Job satisfaction

We argue in Chapter 2 that buying a business can enhance performance in the three principal areas of profitability, growth and risk control. Adverse effects in the other four areas are possible but avoidable.

In Chapter 3 we look at how the management of an existing business or a management buy-out or buy-in team can achieve above average profitability by buying a business. The key is to identify investment, asset strip or turn round prospects. Chapter 3 also deals with other opportunities for improving profitability, growth or risk control which the management of an existing business can pursue by taking over or merging with another business. We summarise in a matrix the circumstances in which to pursue the five different types of acquisition which we distinguish, namely investment, asset strip, turn round, takeover and merger

We move on in Chapters 4 and 5 to discuss the issues and the alternatives which management should consider before confirming that it is wise for them to pursue a strategy of acquisition.

1.3 A FEASIBLE DEAL

A management buy-out team which is committed to the idea of acquiring their business has only to make contact with the potential seller to see if a deal is possible. Most buyers however have a more difficult path in front of them before they get that far.

In Chapter 6, we look at how to use an acquisition profile to shortlist candidates, how to allocate resources to the search process and how to apply the two main methods that are available. The "broker method" involves looking amongst businesses known to be for sale for those which fit the acquisition profile. The "research method" involves looking for businesses which fit the acquisition profile and then seeing if the owners are prepared to sell.

Having contacted a business which fits the acquisition profile and which appears to be for sale at a reasonable price, a potential buyer should not rush into buying without assessing beforehand whether a deal is really feasible. This involves meeting the key people, drawing up an outline agreement and performing a high-level financial appraisal of the acquisition.

1.4 THE BUYING

Once a business has been found which it makes strategic sense to buy, the complex job of managing the buying process begins. The issues are introduced in Chapter 7. It is tempting to present buying a business as a single logical series of tasks but it is impractical to impose a strict order on events. Several activities are in progress at any time and this presents a major challenge to good management and good decision-making.

When trying to make decisions about acquisitions, the would-be buyer is surrounded by individuals and organisations with interests of their own to pursue. There are the target's owners, the target's managers, the professional advisers of both the buyer and the seller, the institutions prepared to finance the acquisition, the Inland Revenue and the regulatory authorities under whose jurisdiction a proposed transaction falls.

Amid the excitement, management must not lose sight of what buying a business is about. Buyers agree to make payments in the form of finance costs, tax bills, professional fees, golden handshakes, post-acquisition investment and, of course, the purchase consideration. They are prepared to make these payments in return for the greater benefits which they expect to derive from the target business. At the same time, buyers need to protect themselves and ensure that they are being provided with complete and accurate information by obtaining assurances from the sellers in the form of warranties and indemnities.

Management's prime objective is to maximise the excess of benefit over cost. If they are satisfied with the excess then they should see to it that neither the seller, nor a rival buyer, nor the regulatory authorities prevent the deal from going ahead. On the other hand, if the best deal that management can secure is not sufficiently advantageous, then they must abort the acquisition. Management should not be propelled into buying because the negotiations have a seemingly unstoppable momentum. There is also no point in carrying on in an attempt to recoup costs that have already been incurred.

We aim to help managers stay in control. We identify major issues of the buying process and examine the principal activities which are used to address them. We deal with six such activities in Chapters 7 to 18 as indicated.

1. Negotiation (7)
2. Valuing the business (8)

3. Structuring the acquisition (9, 10, 11, 12)
4. Securing legal protection (13)
5. Investigating the target (14, 15, 16, 17)
6. Protecting the investor when buying in public (18)

The first activity we consider is negotiation. It is not enough to have an understanding of all the other buying activities. Management have to be able to apply that knowledge in negotiation to conclude an advantageous deal. This involves management "selling" their own acquisition proposals to the sellers.

Next we look at valuation. All buyers should fundamentally be trying to buy a business which is worth more to them than they pay for it. Valuation involves putting a value on a target and using this as an upper price limit. From valuation, we move on to discuss how a worthwhile acquisition can be structured to ensure that the full value of a target is realised and that any shortfalls are properly compensated. The discretion which can be exercised in structuring an acquisition is considerable and should be responsive to the financing, tax planning and accounting objectives of the buyer.

Some of the remaining buying activities are not relevant to all buyers because acquisitions take so many forms. If neither the buyer nor the target is quoted or part of a quoted group, there is no need to comply with regulations to protect public investors. Where the target is a quoted company, the scope for securing legal protection and for investigating the target is minimal. On the other hand, if business assets are bought rather than shares, the need for protection and investigation is reduced because the buyer does not inherit the entire legal and tax history of a target company.

Although management are responsible for the final deal, they normally delegate much of the work of the buying process to specialist advisers. These advisers include accountants, solicitors and, on public company transactions, merchant bankers and stockbrokers. To derive a net benefit from their advisers, management need to be aware of the issues the specialists should address. Chapters 7 to 18 should provide such an awareness. In addition, Appendix II identifies the matters which can be covered by an investigation of a target and Appendix III outlines the warranties and indemnities which solicitors can build into a purchase contract.

After our examination of strategy, search and buying, Chapter 19 points out how these stages are affected when buying abroad.

1.5 MAKING IT A SUCCESS

Management should only buy a business if they have a clear view of what to do with it afterwards. In Chapter 20 we look at initiatives to fulfil the strategic purpose of an acquisition.

An asset strip involves getting on with stripping out the assets. With other acquisitions, management need to pay careful attention to the corporate image and the people of the target business and perhaps to those of their own business too. You have to introduce significant changes to improve the target's performance or to integrate its operations with your own. You have to dispel uncertainty through good communication and motivation skills.

In the aftermath of a deal, managment should also make sure that they reap the full benefits of any legal protection established during the buying process and monitor the success of an acquisition in relation to its original purpose. To review each acquisition and to learn from personal experience are sure but perhaps painful ways of making the next acquisition even more successful.

1.6 FRAMEWORKS OR FIREWORKS?

We have now presented, in outline form, a framework of ideas which we develop throughout the book. We have identified four stages of acquisition activity, seven areas of performance, five types of acquisition, two methods of searching for a target and six activities to co-ordinate when buying a business.

Yet, no matter how disciplined the presentation can be made to seem, events in real life are likely to be more confusing. It usually takes real flair to identify and resolve the issues that arise during the acquisition process. Moreover, some acquisition opportunities require decisions to be made quickly and on the basis of limited information. In short, enthusiasm and fire are needed.

Nevertheless, when the pressure is on, a structured approach to acquisitions should not be abandoned. It is a time instead to delegate and sub-contract whilst checking that the important issues are not overlooked. By sticking to a decision-making framework you impress the sellers and make them more willing to sell to you, you impress the people who are financing the deal, you get better value for money from your advisers and you greatly increase your chances of post-acquisition success.

In this book we concentrate, without apology, on the orderly processes of structured decision-making. Experience suggests that, when it comes to acquisitions, people are inclined to be dazzled by spectacular visions and to forget commercial common sense. As a result, many get their fingers burnt.

2.

STRATEGIC GROUND RULES

2.1 THE NEED FOR STRATEGY

Anyone buying a business should only do so in pursuit of a specific business strategy. This applies equally to managers who are looking to add to their existing business, to stage a buy-out or to buy into another business from a zero base.

For some people, business strategy sounds too pompous or too time-consuming to be taken seriously. Such people have no set views on whether they want to buy a particular business and no preconceptions of how much they might be prepared to pay. They make no particular attempt to seek out an opportunity but are open-minded in considering, on its merits, any opportunity which comes their way.

The views which we have just sketched might sound down-to-earth but they are not particularly pragmatic or efficient and they are unlikely to inspire confidence in anyone who is called upon to finance an acquisition. Such views would also appear peculiar if applied to important private purchases of, for example, a house or a car. It is only sensible to decide what you want to acquire and why, and then to go out and find the best buy. Such an approach is all that is meant by buying a business in pursuit of a specific business strategy.

2.2 BUSINESS OBJECTIVES

Individual managers or management teams need to draw up business strategies which will help them to realise specific objectives. These objectives should not just aim to enhance a manager's own motivation and position, but should also reflect the objectives of others upon whom a manager may depend, such as providers of capital and key employees. Business objectives fall into seven principal areas.

1. Profitability
    Profitability is expressed as a return on capital employed or, in the case of a quoted company, as an earnings per share value which shareholders will not want to see reduced or diluted.
2. Growth.
    Growth may be measured in terms, for example, of turnover, assets, employees and locations.
3. Risk control
    Risk control is the reduction of exposure to uncontrollable external forces.
4. Liquidity
    Liquidity is access to cash to meet day-to-day or long-term business requirements.
5. Dividends
    Dividends are amounts paid to shareholders out of profits.
6. Corporate image
    Corporate image sums up the perceptions which outsiders have of a business and its people, service, expertise and style.
7. Job satisfaction
    Job satisfaction refers to what the people throughout an organisation gain from their employment. Together with corporate image, the practices which determine job satisfaction constitute the "corporate culture" of a business.

2.3 REALISTIC EXPECTATIONS

There are likely to be gaps in the key areas of performance between the expectations which management and others have and the current prospects of the business; a shortfall between where the various audiences believe the business needs to go and where it is presently going. If these gaps cannot be made good by management, then they and others will be disappointed.

Disappointed outside shareholders, lenders and key employees are capable of giving management a rough ride, diminishing their status and effectiveness or, ultimately, removing them from office. The management and indeed the organisation may not survive. Managers can find themselves: removed by their shareholders or subordinates; subject to a takeover which is attractive to disgruntled shareholders; or replaced by a receiver if key lenders lose confidence. Owner-managers can be put out of business altogether.

It is evident that alert management do not allow significant gaps to remain between expectations and prospects. They adopt strategies to narrow the gaps. Like any other business strategy, an acquisition strategy should be rooted in a realistic expectation that it will help to achieve a desired mix of profitability, growth, risk control, liquidity, dividends, corporate image and job satisfaction.

We believe that it is realistic to expect that buying a business can enhance prospects in the three principal performance areas of profitability, growth and risk control. In Chapter 3 we look at how above average profitability can be achieved from investment in another business even where the buyer does not have another existing business to which the acquisition can be added. This is of particular relevance to management buy-outs and management buy-ins. Later on we look at the special opportunities which arise for improving not just profitability but also growth and risk control when an existing business is making an acquisition.

We do not ourselves believe that an acquisition strategy can be justified on the basis of seeking to improve performance in any of the other four performance areas. Nevertheless, management should think through the consequences in these other areas when considering acquisition as a means to improved profitability, growth or risk control.

2.4 ACQUIRING FOR LIQUIDITY?

We need to justify our view that the desire for improved liquidity could not be the driving force behind a coherent acquisition strategy. It might be argued that ambitious businesses often feel that it is unduly difficult to raise funds to finance development. In consequence, they may be persuaded to acquire companies with available cash, access to unused bank facilities or an apparent ability to generate cash earnings. In such cases, acquisition seems to be justified as a means of financing other forms of investment. Why is the argument invalid?

There is a practical peril. Sometimes a potential target does not have the surplus financial resources which it appears to have from its accounts. A company can actually need its "surplus finance" to complete contracts on which it has received advance payments, to handle a seasonal peak in its trade or to fund imminent capital investment requirements.

Accepting however that there is surplus finance, the finance is likely to have been generated by the target's operations. Except with the purest of "cash shell" companies, those operations have to be bought as well even though they are of secondary interest to the would-be buyer of liquidity. For this reason, the whole acquisition exercise can turn in to a very costly lesson for the buyer.

After the acquisition, existing bank facilities may not be renewed. The target's employees may become demoralised at the buyer's lack of interest in the development of the business and the intention of milking it as a "cash cow". Because of low morale and the buyer's inability to understand the business, the target may even start to make losses and absorb cash. In fact, the buyer's investment in the liquidity, the goodwill and the trading assets of the target may be rapidly run down and wasted.

Nevertheless, although the acquisition of liquidity is unlikely to be a good idea, it still appears to be a credible motive in the public arena. Quoted companies who fear that they are likely takeover targets quite often take advantage of a "purchase of own shares" to return excess cash to their shareholders.

2.5 BUYING DIVIDENDS?

Dividends are rarely of interest to owner-managers, but they are often of vital importance to companies with outside shareholders, especially when their shares are quoted. Dividend levels are an important factor in determining the price of quoted shares, the value of a shareholder's investment and the ability of management to raise new finance. In spite of this, a company's dividend prospects can only be fundamentally altered by changes in profitability, growth and risk. An acquisition strategy itself cannot be usefully developed by reference to the ultimate goal of improving dividend prospects.

Nonetheless, can acquisition be attractive, in a cosmetic way, to a company with small distributable resources? Distributable reserves comprise the amounts of profit realised in the past which can be paid out to shareholders by way of dividend. Where these reserves are small and a company is not able to meet outside shareholders' dividend expectations, is it sensible to buy a company with high distributable reserves?

For accounting and legal reasons the envisaged manoeuvre only works if shares in a company are bought almost entirely in exchange for shares in the buying company. In these circumstances, so-called merger accounting principles can be applied and the distributable reserves of the buyer and the target remain largely intact and available for distribution by the buyer. In all other types of acquisition, none of the target company's distributable reserves earned prior to the acquisition are legally available for distribution by the buyer.

Even in circumstances where it is possible to conjure up some distributable reserves through merger accounting, the question remains as to whether such a move has any commercial credibility. If the buyer is going to make profits in the future which will allow it to pay adequate dividends, then it should be able to convince shareholders not to demand dividends now instead of entering into an otherwise unjustified acquisition. On the other hand, if the buyer is not going to make profits in the future which will allow it to pay adequate dividends, then there seems little point in buying a business and running down its assets merely to disguise this fact.

2.6 CORPORATE IMAGE AND ACQUISITION

By corporate image we mean the whole range of facts and impressions which a company's name conjures up in the minds of outsiders, be they suppliers, customers, competitors, job applicants or prospective investors. The term is not only applicable to large media-conscious companies. Even if a business is small or does not have a high public profile, it still has an image within its own markets and localities. It should try to manage that image, for example, by establishing relationships with influential organisations and the local and trade press.

A corporate image is not something imaginary or trivial. It is a large part of what is usually called goodwill and it is especially important in determining people's attitudes towards doing business with a company. Publicity campaigns may be used to reinforce internal efforts to alter attitudes to quality of service and product, change, style, efficiency and competitiveness. Publicity which seeks however to project a corporate image which is inconsistent with the way the business and its people actually operate will after a time merely confuse and discredit.

Can the management of a business use acquisition as a means of bringing about a desired change in corporate image? A company which buys a business in order to change its own image must of necessity buy a business with a different image. Any quick attempt to change one to conform with the other will probably lead to both images becoming confused and the better image may become tarnished. If images are inconsistent then the businesses concerned should generally be allowed to retain their original identity. Acquisition should therefore not be used to upgrade a corporate image.

2.7 ACQUISITION AND JOB SATISFACTION

By job satisfaction we refer to the views of employees as to what they get out of their jobs. It covers remuneration, security, advancement, responsibility, confidence, challenge, esteem and sense of belonging. Job satisfaction is determined by the full range of personnel practices adopted by a business and poor performance may manifest itself in demotivation, indiscipline, poor work, searching for other jobs, resignations or industrial action. It makes sense for management to be interested in realising their own expectations of job satisfaction and those of "key employees".

By key employees we do not just mean people in senior and well-paid positions. We refer instead to all those employees who can cause major problems for management if they are dissatisfied. The quality of a company's selling effort or customer service is often dependent upon the strong motivation of certain employees. Alternatively, some people can behave in a way which is visibly demoralising or disruptive or they can take effective industrial action and mobilise outside opposition. Sometimes people also become key employees because they have skills which are in short supply or because they have some specific experience or technical expertise which it would cost a great deal of time and money to replace.

Is it possible for an acquisition strategy to be justified on the grounds that it will help to realise expectations of job satisfaction? The simple answer is, "No". It is true that many people relish the excitement of the acquisition process and the challenge of an acquisition because it gives them a chance to prove themselves. This applies to management buyouts and buy-ins as well as to acquisitions by existing businesses. Others may see acquisition as a route to improved opportunities or job security.

The objection is that people only have a chance to prove themselves a success or to enjoy new opportunities and security if an acquisition can lead to improvements in the fundamentals of profitability, growth and risk. Unless there is some such justification for acquisition, then the enthusiasts are doomed to failure and disappointment. It is to the real justifications of acquisition that we should turn our attention.

3.

BUYING TO CREATE VALUE

3.1 STAND-ALONE DEALS

Profitability, growth and risk are fundamental to the valuation of any asset. For example, the value of a company share is affected by profits or earnings per share, the anticipated growth in those earnings and the riskiness or uncertainty of the earnings in the future.

A worthwhile and successful acquisition is one which generates a better mix of profitability, growth and risk reduction for the buyer than is reflected in the acquisition price. In these circumstances the acquisition creates value for the buyer because the business is worth more than the price paid. In any acquisition, buy-out or buy-in, this can occur in two situations.

1. Management apply their knowledge and methods to improve upon the performance which is reflected in other people's valuations.
2. The existing owners and other potential buyers do not appreciate the strategic strength of a business, for example because they do not realise how circumstances are about to change in its favour.

In addition, when an existing business buys another, value can be created because of "synergy" between the two businesses. We explain what we mean by this later in the chapter. Firstly though we look at the characteristics of successful acquisitions which are not dependent upon the benefits of synergy with an existing business. We refer to such acquisitions as stand-alone deals.

The successful types of acquisition which we discuss arise because, even without being privy to inside information, a buyer can see a business differently from the sellers and any rival buyers. What looks like an expensive business to one person can look like a bargain to someone else.

A different sort of bargain purchase occurs when a buyer simply has a negotiating advantage over sellers who need to make a quick sale, or who have had no other enquiries or who are poor negotiators. Alternatively, sellers can be prepared to make concessions on price in order to sell to the "right sort" of buyer, such as a buyer with no plans for radically altering the business. Whatever the reasons for this "soft seller" type of bargain purchase, the understandable desire to make such bargain purchases is not an adequate basis for the development of an acquisition strategy.

3.2 ASSET STRIP, TURN ROUND OR INVESTMENT

The prospect of creating value from an acquisition arises where a business is poorly managed. A buyer can improve upon the performance which has been achieved by the seller and which is reflected in the value of the business to the seller. This is sometimes the case with a family business which has not been run with profit and growth in mind: key management posts are occupied by members of the family who are not up to the job and their presence stifles the ambitions and initiative of better qualified employees.

If a number of people spot the potential for improving performance and become rival bidders, the price will rise as more of the benefits of better management are passed on to the seller and the acquisition becomes less valuable to a buyer. Clearly, any bidder should withdraw once the asking price reflects the bidder's estimate of the full potential of the target business. A successful bidder also needs to act particularly quickly afterwards to realise the target's potential and ensure that the acquisition is beneficial overall.

Two courses of action are open to the buyer of a poorly managed business. Which course of action is taken depends largely on the buyer's view of the target's strategic strength. If the target is well positioned in a market with a good future then the buyer should aim to turn the business round. If instead the target business is poorly positioned, perhaps in a stagnant market and with poor products and people, then it usually makes more sense to strip the target. The idea here is to convert the target's poorly used assets into cash. The alternatives are not mutually exclusive and an asset strip of part of a target can help fund a turn round of the remainder of the business. Indeed there is an element of asset stripping in any acquisition insofar as a buyer sees an opportunity to sell off surplus assets.

Opportunities for creating value through acquisition also arise when a buyer sees strategic strength in a business which is not fully appreciated by the sellers or potential rival buyers. In such cases the action taken after the acquisition depends on the perceived quality of the management. Where this is good there is little point in interfering and the buyer should adopt a "hands off" management style, regarding the target as an investment. Where management is considered poor, the turn round approach is again necessary.

The argument so far about stand-alone deals can be summarised in the matrix shown below. We will extend the matrix later in this chapter to incorporate synergy-based deals.

	Quality of target's past management		
	Good	Poor but potential reflected in price	Poor and potential not reflected in price
Strength of target's strategic position			
Poor	No deal	No deal	Asset strip
Good but reflected in price	No deal	No deal	Turn round
Good and not reflected in price	Investment	Turn round	Turn round

The full strategic strength of a target and the potential for improving on past management performance only come to be reflected in the asking price as a result of either astute negotiation by the sellers or a process of rival bidding.

3.3 STRATEGIC MOVES

It should go without saying from our argument so far that there is no point in buying any business at a price which reflects in full both the buyer's view of its underlying strength and performance levels which the buyer could not better.

There are however situations where people appear quite willing to buy into strategically well positioned businesses even when a full price has to be paid. In these cases, buyers seem to see growth or risk control as objectives in themselves which can be used to justify an acquisition even if no value is created. Perhaps the target's market is seen as offering a strong base for the successful pursuit of a broad range of business objectives. Depending upon the quality of the target's existing management, such "strategic move" acquisitions can be classified as highly priced variants of the investment or the turn round.

In general, we are sceptical of the advisability of such acquisitions, except where the benefits clearly exceed the costs. The arguments for strategic moves in pursuit of growth or risk reduction do however merit attention.

3.4 ACQUISITION AND THE LIMITS TO GROWTH

Acquisition can be used to overcome key constraints which face any management team trying to enter new and strategically attractive markets. Such "stepping stone acquisitions" can allow growth to proceed at an otherwise unimagined pace.

Constraints on growth arise because of management's inexperience in new areas of business. Management often realise that they cannot sustain growth without venturing into new markets and countries and introducing new products and distribution channels, but progress needs to be cautious and growth slow due to inexperience. Buying a business involves buying management with experience and expertise in a new market.

Growth can also be frustrated because of barriers to entry into new markets, such as the lack of an established reputation, a distribution network or some manufacturing know-how. Acquisition is a means of overcoming such barriers. Management buy-in teams may also see the acquisition of a quoted company as a quick way of overcoming barriers to entry into the Stock Market. Indeed, they may be ready to pay a very full price so that they can issue paper for future acquisitions instead of waiting to build up and float a new business.

The inability of the management pyramid to match the desired growth rate of a business is a further brake on growth. The risks of too fast a growth rate are that individual managers are promoted beyond their level of competence or find their areas of responsibility or their numbers of immediate subordinates increasing out of control. When a business grows by acquiring another it acquires the target's management hierarchy. Whilst some of the target's managers are likely not to "fit" in the enlarged organisation, the strain put on external recruitment and internal promotion is at least reduced.

A final limit on growth, in the absence of acquisition, is that an individual company can only grow by being highly competent and competitive. Either it must be quick to identify and enter new growth markets or it must fight it out in established markets. Fighting it out involves increasing total market capacity and then taking customers away from competitors. Acquisition offers a more assured prospect of expansion; it offers growth apparently without tears.

3.5 REDUCING RISK THROUGH ACQUISITION

People use the word risk to mean two very different things. Firstly, they mean vulnerability to favourable and unfavourable fluctuations caused by uncontrollable factors. Secondly, they use the word to refer to "the downside", the chance that things will take a catastrophic and lasting turn for the worse; we refer to such risks as threats. Markets which are characterised by low risk of both sorts are strategically attractive and managers may be prepared to pay a full price to enter them.

Such acquisitions are particularly tempting to managers with existing businesses which are strategically unattractive because they are threatened. There are many types of threats: a product may be made technically obsolete; an industry may become socially unacceptable; a source of supply may dry up; the prospect of low-cost, large-scale foreign production may endanger a business; or a company may even fear being acquired.

Threat reduction generally involves moving out of the activity which is endangered and moving in to less dangerous areas. Acquisition is a quick way of doing this. Cases of threat reduction include diversifying out of cigarette manufacture or setting up production operations in export markets which could otherwise become inaccessible because of protectionism or the high cost of domestic production. Non-EEC businesses who fear exclusion from a Single European Market may view acquisition as a means of addressing this threat. Nonetheless, those who seek to acquire in order to reduce risk should remember that acquisition is a risky business. It is especially risky when it involves venturing into new and poorly understood industries and countries. There is also little long-term safety to be gained from mere size and variety.

Although the risk-reducing acquisitions we have been considering are of most interest to people with unattractive existing businesses, they are essentially stand-alone deals since no links are forged between the existing business and the target. We now move on to consider acquisitions where such links are forged, including acquisitions which involve reducing exposure to our first "vulnerability" type of risk.

3.6 TWO PLUS TWO EQUALS FIVE?

Whereas the management buy-out or buy-in team typically have no existing business to which to add an acquisition target, other buyers do. An existing business provides an additional opportunity for a buyer to create value through acquisition and this can have the effect of pushing the price beyond the reach of other potential buyers. The reason for this is synergy.

The concept of synergy is grandly paraphrased as "the whole is greater than the sum of the parts" and is captured in the formula "2 + 2 = 5". The term is sometimes viewed with suspicion since it can be used as a vague blanket justification for ill-conceived acquisitions. Businesses also face some stiff challenges if they are to make synergy work. Consequently, the premium that people are prepared to pay for synergy is likely to be limited.

Nevertheless, there are genuine circumstances in which synergy can arise and in which two businesses can achieve together what is beyond their individual capabilities. Profitability, growth and risk reduction can all be improved through synergy.

3.7 PROFIT FROM SYNERGY

From an austere analytical standpoint, there are three ways in which a trading business can increase the profitability of its operations, whether profitability is measured as a return on capital employed or as earnings per share, which is the appropriate measure of profitability for a quoted company.

1. Capital economies arise from an improvement in the ratio of sales to net assets.
2. Overhead economies reflect a reduction in the ratio of overheads to sales.
3. Contribution economies lead to an increase in gross margin or the ratio of gross profit to sales.

Where the three ways to improved profitability are associated with an increased size of operations they are covered by the term "economies of scale". Increased size is a consequence of acquisition and so economies of scale can be used to justify synergy-based deals. The scope for economies of scale within Europe is likely to increase as moves are made to reduce internal barriers to trade: this will provide a new impetus for synergy-based deals. In all cases however it needs to be shown that after an acquisition the ratios we have identified are better than would be expected on the basis of adding together figures for the buyer and the target.

Capital economies of scale involve an increase in the ratio of sales to net assets. Opportunities for achieving such economies through acquisition arise when a business is stuck with underused fixed assets. Successful acquisitions inspired by capital economies mean that greatly increased volumes of business are, for example, put through an existing computer facility, a process plant or the warehouses and transport fleet of a distribution network. In addition, underutilised intangible assets such as trade names and know-how, which are often not recognised in a firm's accounts, provide a basis for profitable acquisition.

An acquisition might improve not only the ratio of sales to fixed assets but also the ratio of sales to working capital. Increased power over suppliers and customers gives scope for the slower payment of creditors and the faster collection of debts. Increased power allows greater influence to be exercised over the timing of both the despatch and receipt of goods and so reduces the levels of stock that need to be held.

Overhead economies of scale occur when profit margins are improved because of a reduction in the ratio of overheads to sales. Perhaps the most dramatic instances of overhead economies are those which can occur when high technology businesses merge and rationalise their research and development activities. Furthermore, profitability improves as it becomes economic to take on higher quality specialist staff: an enlarged business can keep them occupied and motivated and enjoy the benefits of their skills.

Overheads also include financing costs. An increased scale of operations gives a company more bargaining power with lenders and access to new and cheaper sources of finance. Additional opportunities for overhead economies usually arise in conjunction with the capital economies of scale already described. For example, the running costs associated with operating previously underutilised fixed assets can be spread over a greater volume of business.

The term "contribution" refers to the difference between the value of sales and the costs directly attributable to those sales. Contribution economies of scale lead to the improvement of profit margins through a fall in the ratio of direct costs to sales. Economies result either from increases in selling prices or from reductions in direct costs, whether through lower buying prices or improved efficiency.

An acquisition enables increased selling prices and lower buying prices to be obtained because of the greater bargaining power of an enlarged business. Acquisitions are commonly followed by the renegotiation of discounts and rebates with suppliers and in wholesale and retail trades this is often a significant feature of an acquisition.

The alternative cause of contribution economies of scale, namely improved efficiency, is normally associated with manufacturing industry. Greater labour productivity and reduced usage of materials are advantages which can follow on from an acquisition if production runs are longer and the scope for specialisation is increased. The concept of the "learning curve" is also relevant. Increased experience of a manufacturing process, as measured by cumulative production volumes, brings with it significant unit cost savings. Nevertheless, it is worth asking if acquisition is diverting resources away from other investments which are more likely to generate such economies. For example, would the expansion of an existing plant generate greater learning curve and other savings than the acquisition of somebody else's plant?

3.8 SYNERGY AND GROWTH

Acquisition can be used to produce instant growth in terms of turnover, total assets, employees, locations, product range, market share, industry spread or geographical coverage. If the growth is of the "2 + 2 = 4" variety, it merely reflects the fact that the target's turnover, total assets and so on are added to the buyer's and so the buyer becomes bigger.

Nonetheless, acquisitions lead to growth "with synergy" where the buyer's existing products are sold into the target's customer base and the target's products are sold to the buyer's customers in ways which would not be possible without an acquisition. Growth with synergy is being invoked whenever it is argued that an acquisition leads to a broader range of complementary products and services being made available to customers who prefer "one stop shopping".

For example, suppose a road building firm finds that part of the road building market is not open to it because some of its potential customers want to buy bridges to go with their roads and they want to buy both their roads and their bridges from the same contractor. In this case, if the road building firm finds a bridge building firm in a situation which mirrors its own, there is scope for the two of them jointly to increase their shares of both the road market and the bridge market. Looking at it another way, by joining together, the two firms can enter the combined road and bridge market. Here quite definitely "2 + 2 = 5", although it should be noted that in many sectors the trend is towards specialised "niche markets" rather than one stop shopping.

3.9 BALANCED RISKS

In considering stand-alone deals earlier we introduced two types of risk: vulnerability to fluctuations and the chance that things will get worse. In discussing synergy, we concentrate on the first sort of risk.

It is generally assumed that most people prefer to have less rather than more of the first type of risk. They would not be happy if, at the end of the month, their employer offered to toss a coin on the basis of heads no salary, tails double salary. Consequently, people try to reduce such risk. If somebody made a second offer to the effect that, on the same toss of the coin, heads meant receiving an amount equal to salary and tails meant losing such an amount, people would not mind accepting the two offers together as they would then always be certain of getting their salary.

Many managements, outside · shareholders, lenders and key employees see the current business in which they are involved as exposed to variability which they do not like. Accordingly, some managements seek to acquire a business as a way of reducing variability. The acquisition strategy is that of the sunglasses seller looking to buy an umbrella seller. If the strategy succeeds then the results of the business will be similar whether it rains or shines. Synergy is involved here since two risky businesses have been combined to produce one low-risk business. As well as the weather, interest rate fluctuations, commodity price changes, fashions and currency movements can give rise to variability in a company's performance. In these cases too, businesses can be acquired to balance the risks involved.

Care must be taken to make sure that a strategy of balancing risks through acquisition does not degenerate into a shopping spree and result in a ragbag of poorly understood and poorly matched companies. It should also be realised that certain outside lenders and shareholders prefer to balance their own risks. They prefer to invest in a sunglasses seller who understands the sunglasses market and an umbrella seller who understands the umbrella market instead of seeing their investment in a sunglasses business being jeopardised by a foray into the unknown world of umbrellas.

3.10 TAKEOVERS AND MERGERS

We have seen the opportunities an existing business has to enhance its profitability, growth and risk control by generating synergy through acquisition. Success depends on not paying a price which swallows up all the benefits of synergy. It also depends on combining and co-ordinating the functions of the two businesses in the areas where synergy gains are anticipated.

Earlier in this chapter we saw that in stand-alone deals the quality of the target management affected the style of an acquisition and meant the difference between taking a "hands off" investment approach or carrying out a turn round or an asset strip. The quality of the target management is equally important where synergy is at stake.

If target management is poor, little is lost by "taking over" the running of the acquired business and forcing the pace on realising synergy gains. Where target management is good however, then such an approach is demotivating and probably reduces the value of the acquisition and the chances of succeeding in achieving synergy gains. In these circumstances the acquisition needs to be viewed as a merger and the two entities should be fused together.

We are now in a position to extend the previous matrix to summarise our arguments on synergy-based deals. The full chart is reproduced in Appendix I.1. as the Acquisition Type Matrix.

	Quality of target's past management		
	Good	Poor but potential reflected in price	Poor and potential not reflected in price
Strength of target's strategic position			
Scope for synergy reflected in price	No deal	No deal	Takeover
Scope for synergy not reflected in price	Merger	Takeover	Takeover

The scope for improving on past management performance and for realising synergy gains will only be reflected in the asking price because of the negotiating skills of sellers or the competitive bidding of other potential buyers.

As with stand-alone deals, some managements decide to pay a full price in order to make an acquisition which they regard as being a sound strategic move. The justification of such takeovers and mergers is suspect although in real life they are likely to be disguised by the over-optimistic appraisal of either the strategic potential of a business or the benefits of new management.

4.

WILL ACQUISITION WORK?

4.1 RISKS AND OPPORTUNITIES

The business objectives of profitability, growth and risk control can be furthered by buying a business. In this chapter we consider the critical judgements which managers need to make in deciding whether the strategy of buying a business will actually work for them.

The aim is not merely to highlight the risks of wrongly deciding to pursue acquisitions. It is just as unfortunate to err on the side of caution and miss an opportunity as it is to make an ill-advised acquisition. The aim is not to avoid risk but to manage it by being aware of the issues.

In the initial stage of formulating strategy, issues arise from three sources.

1. The Acquisition Type Matrix developed in Chapter 3 which distinguished five types of acquisition: asset strip, turn round, investment, takeover and merger.
2. Effects on liquidity, dividends, corporate image and job satisfaction
3. Competition law

4.2 DO YOU REALLY UNDERSTAND?

Our five types of acquisition are distinguished by the different circumstances in which they are appropriate and the different management actions which need to follow. Crucial however to the ability to identify any acquisition opportunity and to handle it properly is the ability to understand the target's industry.

The need for an appreciation of the target's strategic strength and prospects is essential for all types of acquisition and it raises a fundamental doubt about buying businesses in unfamiliar industries. An acquisition turns into a catastrophe if for example the barriers to entry, which justified a high price, suddenly collapse. In general, a management team that is about to make an acquisition should have a broad range of skills covering the buying, production, marketing, distribution and technical demands of the target's industry.

An understanding of a target's industry is a prerequisite for evaluating the past performance of the target: Such an ability is required for any acquisition, since it is the basis for identifying and realising the future potential of a business and arriving at an appropriate valuation. Anyone staging a management buy-out or making a friendly acquisition of a private company normally has plenty of information upon which to base an assessment. Others need to have sharper skills if they are to come to the right conclusions on limited information.

A management team must understand a target's industry and its past performance before making any acquisition. In takeovers and mergers by an existing business, management must also understand their own business. Because synergy is expected to result from the combination of the buyer and the target, it will be embarrassing and wasteful if trends in the buyer's technology or market place limit the scope for synergy in the future.

4.3 CAN YOU DO IT IN PRACTICE?

As well as being able to understand businesses and so identify acquisition opportunities, potential buyers also need to know how to take advantage of the opportunities they see and create value from an acquisition. Where the target's management is seen as poor and the buyer intends to replace it, as in the turn round and the takeover, particular abilities are required. The buyer needs to know how to apply corrective management skills and must be prepared to take difficult decisions to get rid of inadequate or surplus employees and bad business practices.

The ability to shake a business up and turn it round is not the same as that required to run a business in a more stable environment. The management of a potential buyer must be candid about whether they have the experience and the "stomach" for the job. If they have not, then their subsequent inaction or misdirected actions will mean that they do not realise the improved profits of an intended turn round or the synergy of a takeover.

Nevertheless, in a takeover by an existing business, the target's operations do not just need "sorting out". Management also require another sort of skill. It is the skill which is required on its own in our merger type of acquisition. In a merger, the target is well managed but its operations need to be absorbed into the new combined entity. These circumstances call for subtle skills of integration and conciliation. If management lack the skills or the inclination to act appropriately, they should steer clear of both takeovers and mergers because they will not reap the benefits of synergy which they anticipate.

So far we have identified the qualities which managers should look for in themselves before embarking upon an acquisition strategy aimed at realising improvements in profitability, growth and risk control. However, a management team which has the skills to make a success of a particular type of acquisition should not necessarily pursue such acquisitions. No doubt many retailers could successfully acquire many of their suppliers, but if they are actually better at retailing than at manufacturing, then they should stick to that.

A management which is keen to pursue profitability, growth and risk control through acquisition should also not lose sight of other business objectives, including liquidity, dividends, corporate image and job satisfaction. Although they are not sufficient reasons in themselves for embarking upon an acquisition strategy, they may justify not embarking upon apparently attractive acquisitions.

4.4 PRESERVING LIQUIDITY AND DIVIDENDS

A fundamental threat to any acquisition strategy is that, when it is ill-conceived, the targets become a drain on the buyer's resources and a brake on its profitability. In these circumstances, adverse effects on liquidity and dividends are inevitable.

The effects are even worse if the acquisition strategy is poorly presented at the outset to lenders and shareholders. This makes it more difficult to fund the acquisition adequately in the first place and to generate a reserve of goodwill and understanding to see management through any trying times that lie ahead.

Therefore at the time of formulating an acquisition strategy, a key task is to ensure that the proposed scale of acquisition activity is capable of being adequately funded at an acceptable cost and that those who will be required to provide the funding are supportive of what the buyer is intending to achieve. An acquisition strategy cannot be drawn up in isolation without considering how it is viewed by those who will be called upon to finance it.

4.5 RESPECTING THE CORPORATE IMAGE

Corporate image objectives can come in to conflict with an otherwise well founded acquisition strategy for an established business. Management should avoid targets with corporate images which, in terms of reputation, quality and tradition, are inconsistent with that of the buying company. Differences in corporate image between the buyer and the target may generate a situation of negative synergy or "2 + 2 = 3" which cancels out the intended positive synergy of a takeover or merger. A case in point would be where a high price high quality business buys a low price low quality business. Both individual businesses may lose custom. The buyer may become associated with low quality, the target with high prices. Such dangers do not necessarily invalidate an acquisition strategy, but they do call for selectivity in pursuing the strategy.

The pursuit of an asset strip, a turn round or a takeover requires an unsentimental style of corrective management. Is such a style inconsistent with a buyer's actual or intended corporate image as, for example, a steady, friendly and close-knit family? If so, it is unlikely that such acquisitions can be carried through successfully and without doing long-term damage to the buyer.

Indeed, some companies have such a strong corporate image that they are almost incapable of any effective form of acquisition. They exhibit a fanatical commitment to maintaining consistent and reliable quality of service through unity of purpose, central control and common methods of operation and presentation. Such a business is likely to incur heavy costs in carrying through an acquisition because of its compulsion to make any business it acquires conform with its own monolithic image. These costs must be taken into account when determining the net benefit likely to result from an acquisition.

Nevertheless, we must emphasise that an energetic strategy of acquisition can be used to build a corporate image of success, growth and dynamism. Even those who might attract the slur and stigma of being asset strippers and "hatchet men" may instead manage to portray themselves as agents of necessary economic change, reallocating resources to those best able to use them efficiently and reinvigorating previously neglected businesses.

4.6 MAINTAINING JOB SATISFACTION

Just as a strategy of acquisition can strengthen a company's image if it is well-managed, it can also enhance the job satisfaction of employees by offering good opportunities for ambitious and imaginative employees to prove themselves. In addition, the growth and size that acquisition brings are likely to reinforce the confidence, prestige and status of managers and key employees.

A business which is acquisitive is nonetheless bound to engender uncertainty amongst employees. The uncertainty will arise both when acquisitions are in the offing and, in the wake of an acquisition, when there is uncertainty as to its success and the likelihood of redundancies in the buyer and the target. Such uncertainty can be regarded as good or bad. Management can see it either as keeping everyone on their toes or as distracting people from the main work of the organisation. Others can see it either as providing challenges and opportunities for rapid advancement or as threatening their livelihood.

The characteristics of each particular organisation determine whether the effects of this uncertainty are on balance favourable or adverse and, as a result, whether acquisition is more or less attractive. There is no single right answer. It is up to management to decide whether the sort of acquisition strategy they propose pursuing fits in with the way that they and their employees think.

Management should also be wary of buying target companies which operate very different practices in areas of personnel policy such as recruitment, remuneration, pensions, promotion and consultation. Initially, a proposed acquisition can generate a hostile response from the target's employees and, if it is not too late, an attempt at a management or employee buy-out. Later on, the different practices will be compared and the triumph of one system over the other or a compromise between the two can lead to costly dissatisfaction and even the loss of key employees. Additional costs also result from improving working conditions, pay structures or pension arrangements in the acquired company or the acquiring company, so as to harmonise practices across the enlarged business.

4.7 COMPETITION LAW

We have looked at the issues involved in deciding which of our five types of acquisition is appropriate and in identifying conflicts amongst our seven business objectives. We now consider our final source of issues at the strategy stage . In formulating an acquisition strategy you must allow for competition law.

Often the synergy which drives a takeover or merger is achieved through increased bargaining power. However, those acquisitions which are likely to lead to greater bargaining power are also likely to arouse the fears of competitors, suppliers, customers, the public and the government. The fears are of a growth in monopolistic power leading to higher prices and restricted output. At the expense of everybody else, above average performance will be achieved by the acquirer or will be frittered away in inefficiency. The consequence of such monopoly fears in the United Kingdom is that the Secretary of State for Trade and Industry may, on the advice of the Office of Fair Trading, refer an acquisition to the Monopolies and Mergers Commission.

If a referral is made, the Commission considers whether the proposed transaction is against the public interest. On the basis of the Commission's findings, the Secretary of State, who can prevent, modify or reverse a transaction, makes a decision. At best, a referral involves a frustrating and expensive limbo period of official investigation. In the past this has lasted about six months although strong efforts are being made to reduce the time so that the risk of a referral does not of itself make a potential acquisition too unattractive to pursue. At worst, if an acquisition is prevented, then money, time and effort will have been wasted on the development of an acquisition strategy and the pursuit of a target.

An acquisition is exposed to the risk of referral to the Commission if the value of assets taken over exceeds £30 million or if the resulting business has 25 per cent or more of a national or regional market. Nevertheless, of the transactions which could be referred to the Commission, very few are actually referred.

The selection process is hard to predict and could be influenced by political pressures. The powers of referral have been exercised with differing degrees of enthusiasm and latitude by different governments and ministers. Although the public interest is usually interpreted in competition terms, some referrals are not entirely rooted in a concern for the level of UK competition. Referrals may be made because it is feared that key national assets and industries are passing out of domestic control or are being endangered because of the ambitious financing techniques used by a buyer.

In advance of committing resources to an acquisition strategy, a would-be buyer should, with appropriate advice, assess the dangers of competition law in the light of recent government statements and actions. In addition, confidential guidance from the Office of Fair Trading will indicate whether or not a specific acquisition is likely to be referred to the Commission. The value of this guidance is limited because it is based on just one "side of the story" and is not binding. A new system is being introduced so that buyers can pre-notify transactions to the Office of Fair Trading and avoid a reference by entering into undertakings, for example to sell some of the target's operations.

There are risks not just from UK law but also from EEC legislation and the competition laws of all the countries where the buyer and any target operate. The EEC risks arise if an acquisition affects the coal or steel industries or if it leads either to a reduction in EEC competition or to the abuse of a dominant position. The effect of an acquisition on EEC competition deserves particular attention. The European Commission has been using its considerable powers of regulation with increased vigour and it is likely that the powers of national competition authorities will be supplanted by those of the EEC as part of the movement towards a Single European Market. In particular, the EEC could develop a system for referring and pre-notifying acquisitions.

4.8 RESPONDING TO THE CHALLENGES

In this chapter, we have identified the following issues that may need to be resolved before embarking on an acquisition strategy.

1. Do you really understand the target industry?
2. Do you really understand how to assess management in the target industry and could you manage in that industry?
3. If you propose to buy poorly managed businesses, do you have the skills to sort them out?
4. Can you preserve and integrate the good aspects of a target?
5. Are you sure you know your existing business and where its market is heading?
6. Is your acquisition strategy likely to be frustrated by competition law?
7. Can you find backers for your acquisition plans and keep them happy?
8. Is your corporate image consistent with your acquisition targets and plans and will your acquisition strategy enhance your corporate image?
9. Will your acquisitions involve you in costly changes in employment practices and loss of motivation in your existing business or your targets?

It must be said that the difficulties relating to integration (4), competition law (6), corporate image (8) and job satisfaction (9) are not so relevant to management buy-out and buy-in teams. This tends to redress the balance when such potential buyers are competing against existing businesses who can afford to pay more for potential synergy gains.

Nevertheless, any management team which is considering acquisition is likely to find some of our questions searching. They ought to be confident of their solutions before they become embroiled in the process of identifying or negotiating a deal. The issues are summarised in Appendix I.3 in our Issues Management Guide.

There are three possible responses: research the issue (1, 2, 5 and 6), buy the necessary skills (1, 2, 3, 4, 5 and 6) or, when faced by any of the problems, change the strategy. The acquisition strategy can be changed in detail by, for example, including more specific requirements as to the type of business to be bought. Otherwise, acquisition can be abandoned altogether. Indeed, even those who see acquisition as offering great opportunities and no significant drawbacks should still consider the alternatives.

5.

ALTERNATIVES

5.1 WHAT ARE THE OPTIONS?

There are four types of alternative to buying a controlling interest in a target business.

1. Take less than a controlling interest
2. If you believe that you and the target can benefit each other, enter into a trading relationship
3. Build your own rival business
4. Invest in something else which will give a similar benefit to you as acquiring the target business

For all buyers and all types of acquisition, these choices remain the same. Their practicality and prevalence vary although they can be seen as less exciting than buying a business. Most academic studies show that the gains from acquisition are small and that the principal beneficiaries are the sellers. Even if management think that this is of little relevance to them, they should at least remember that buying a business will preclude them from using their time and resources on some other initiative. It is worth reflecting on the opportunities that are being missed.

We examine some of the main choices in this chapter but we do not consider the numerous options available under the fourth heading given above. Nonetheless, a potential buyer should think creatively about alternative investments. For example, a business which is contemplating a takeover or merger which has risk reduction as its object should remember that a whole variety of hedging transactions can be undertaken with the same end in view. These transactions include insurance arrangements, forward contracts and options of ever-increasing sophistication and flexibility. Although a would-be buyer may be daunted by such financial products, they are unlikely to have the uncertain and potentially disruptive long-term consequences of a business acquisition.

5.2 STAND-ALONE ALTERNATIVES

There are three sorts of acquisition whose rationale does not depend on the combination of the target with a buyer's existing business. They are the asset strip, the turn round and the investment. Such acquisitions are worthwhile because the buyer identifies a gap between the asking price and the potential value of the target. The gap arises because the target has been poorly managed or its strategic strength is not fully recognised.

Such stand-alone acquisitions are the province of managers with specific industry or "company doctor" skills and, unless such managers wish to embark upon a start-up in their preferred sector, the only real alternatives to acquiring a controlling interest of 51 per cent or more in a target business are to take a smaller "slice of the action" or to find another target. The "action" in question is any increase in the value of the target. The smaller slice could involve taking a non-controlling interest or, in the case of an asset strip or turn round, selling specific skills to the target, for example on a consultancy basis.

A reason for taking a more limited role in such stand-alone deals might arise because the situation is considered too risky. Potential buyers might also be uncertain of either their understanding of the target's industry and its past performance or their ability to effect the necessary changes. Alternatively, they may not be able to raise the necessary finance for outright acquisition, or the existing owners may not wish to relinquish control completely.

Nevertheless, these alternatives represent tactical differences in pursuing particular target businesses and do not represent fundamental changes in a strategy of looking for acquisition opportunities to match specific industry knowledge and management skills.

One special case of the stand-alone deal which does merit further attention is the management buy-out. Typically a buy-out team will take a significant interest but not necessarily a controlling interest in the company which buys the target business. This interest will usually exceed both the 10 per cent level at which shareholders can convene an extraordinary general meeting and the 25 per cent level which is needed to block special resolutions. Special resolutions are needed, for example, to change a company's articles of association or its name or to put it into voluntary liquidation. What are the alternatives which face a management team which is considering a buy-out?

5.3 CHOICES FOR THE BUY-OUT TEAM

A management buy-out is often a turn round acquisition motivated by dissatisfaction. Management are unlikely to be too critical of their own past performance but they should see opportunities for running the business they work for better, if they assume ownership. The reasons can include their own improved motivation, the removal of the influence of conservative or distant shareholders and the elimination of unnecessary group overheads.

In addition, buy-outs can be more like the investment type of acquisition. Sometimes, management believe that the present owners are not even aware of the strength of a business because it simply gets lost in group reporting procedures. There have also been well-publicised cases of entrepreneurs who have bought the businesses they floated back from the public. Such entrepreneurs think that the market does not appreciate the strategic strength of their businesses and therefore they believe that the businesses can be bought back from the public for less than their true worth.

The aspirations of a buy-out team are likely to be more specific than for other stand-alone dealmakers. It is the business that they work for and know that they want to buy because they can see the specific opportunities in that business for doing things better and creating value.

The alternative of remaining an employee and simply selling services to the target is obvious but probably unattractive. Other alternatives are nevertheless available. Non-controlling interests can be achieved through share incentive and share option schemes, share purchases on a flotation or other arrangements such as a sponsored spin-out where the business becomes jointly owned by the former owners, management and outside investors. These options can even be more attractive than a buy-out if the risk or the financing requirements of the business are too daunting.

Management should also appreciate that they are sometimes in a position to force the pace on such alternatives, even where the existing shareholders are unwilling to give up power. There is the ultimate threat of staging a so-called management walk-out and either buying an alternative business or pursuing the third major alternative to acquisition, that of starting their own rival business. Such threats should however only be made if they are really credible and also if they do not put management in breach of their service contracts or the duties which some of them will have as directors.

5.4 PIECEMEAL INVESTMENT

Having looked at alternatives to stand-alone deals, we turn to consider alternatives to takeovers and mergers, the synergy-based deals undertaken by existing businesses. Instead of acquiring an entire ready-made business, management could pursue a policy of piecemeal investment and spend directly on research and development, recruitment, training and new capacity. Piecemeal investment can improve trading profitability through capital, overhead and contribution economiess and it can be used to enter new markets and achieve growth and risk reduction. Companies face a "make or buy" decision which is common to many aspects of investment.

Through piecemeal investment management can avoid the often significant professional costs of aborted and completed acquisitions and many of the pitfalls of an acquisition strategy. The pitfalls include Monopolies and Mergers Commission referrals, tough decisions on post-takeover cutbacks and closures, reduced liquidity, delicate post-merger integration, threatened dividends, dangers to a company's image and disruptions to established prospects for job satisfaction. Piecemeal investment can also be eligible for government grants and other forms of assistance which are highly unlikely to be forthcoming for an acquisition.

On the other hand, an acquisition strategy can have important advantages over piecemeal investment as a means to improving trading profitability and growth. Piecemeal investment, unlike acquisition, usually requires an increase in total market capacity and a subsequent battle to ensure that it is competitors who end up with underutilised assets.

Acquisition has advantages when management need to act with speed. We do not deny that a real improvement in trading profitability only materialises through tough decisions and hard bargaining once a business has been bought. A strategy of acquisition is still dramatic and immediately visible to outsiders.

Furthermore, take the case of management who want to increase sales in order to improve asset utilisation and bargaining power. They may face obstacles which cannot be overcome by piecemeal investment in product innovation, market research or advertising. Suppose that they need to be on a particular approved supplier list or have a long-established brand name. In such circumstances, management can justifiably decide to pursue an acquisition strategy to obtain key resources or overcome other barriers to their entry into new markets or market segments.

Risk-reducing diversification is also likely to require entry into activities unfamiliar to existing management. Acquisition involves taking on board a management team who are familiar with the new activity, thereby making major blunders less likely than under a policy of piece-meal investment on an equal scale.

It depends on individual circumstances whether the the limitations of piecemeal investment are serious. It may be feasible to rely on the organic growth such investment generates if growth expectations are modest and can be economically achieved in existing markets.

A benefit of relying on organic growth is that it avoids many of the troubles which can beset a company's image as a result of pursuing a hel-ter skelter policy of aggressive acquisition. In short, the growth appears much more solid. Moreover, under organic growth, the prospects for advancement within the organisation look very attractive to certain employees. The management pyramid will inevitably be getting bigger without there being major injections of "acquired" people.

5.5 COLLABORATION AND SYNERGY

We use the term collaboration to cover arrangements which involve a potential buyer and target entering into a special trading relationship or relinquishing non-controlling share interests. Collaboration can be used to generate synergy in terms of profitability, growth and risk con-trol. Like takeovers and mergers, collaborative arrangements can improve trading profitability through capital, overhead and contribu-tion economies of scale.

The utilisation of fixed assets can be increased by entering into a manufacturing agreement to help meet some of the production require-ments of a company which is short of capacity. Furthermore, manage-ment can increase the utilisation of intangible fixed assets, such as know-how, tradenames and product designs, through franchising or by licensing their use by other companies which operate in markets outside those with which management are familiar. Collaborative arrangements in research and development are also likely to be viewed favourably by government and they may qualify for financial assistance.

More efficient asset utilisation in turn leads to reductions in the ratio of overheads to sales and there is additional scope for dramatic reduc-tions, for example as a result of joint ventures in research and develop-ment. Finally, improved ratios of contribution to sales can be achieved if companies co-operate to form powerful buying and selling consortia.

The usefulness of collaboration in achieving growth depends very much on the type of collaboration agreement involved and the measure of growth used. For example, if collaboration involves making surplus production capacity available to another business, the impact on the apparent size of an organisation may be small and the accounts may only reflect processing and handling charges for the work done.

Alternatively, a manufacturer who sets up an agreement with a distributor may find turnover, number of outlets, public visibility and production capacity greatly increasing. Collaboration can also be particularly important in allowing growth with synergy when consortia or joint marketing arrangements are set up to bring together complementary products and services. Yet even where significant growth is achieved, the risk that collaborative agreements will not be renewed can make the growth seem insecure.

Just as acquisition allows faster growth than piecemeal investment, so collaboration allows still faster growth. This is particularly noticeable in the case of franchising which has allowed fast food restaurants, specialist retailers and small scale service outlets to achieve rapid national and even international coverage. The franchisor simply allows an independent business to trade using the franchisor's own specific and successful corporate culture. In return, the franchisee pays a royalty or has to buy goods and services from the franchisor.

Drawbacks can arise for the franchisor in policing the use of the corporate image, to ensure that it does not become devalued, and in recruiting and maintaining a team of franchisees who are successful and financially sound but who require a minimum investment of time and money from the franchisor. The franchisor must also try to remain highly aware of market trends despite being somewhat removed from the ultimate customer. In addition, while visible growth in terms of outlets may be great, the franchising operation can still look small in its accounts if these only reflect the royalty income generated by the outlets rather than their turnover.

From the other side of the fence, becoming a franchisee can be a useful way of achieving growth. The franchisee buys a ready-made business with a strong corporate image, good training and the benefits of bulk buying discounts. However, the principal drawbacks arise from the fact that the franchisee is forever working within the constraints of the franchisor's corporate culture.

Moving on from growth to risk control, there are numerous circumstances where collaborative ventures can be used as a means of controlling variability and minimising threats. Take the case of businesses which need to develop into new product areas or new countries in order to limit their exposure to chance factors. Often they do not have the expertise or time to go it alone through piecemeal investment and do not have the opportunity to acquire.

Alternatively, a firm whose product range is marketed under a reputable name and distributed through an established network, can find itself threatened by technical developments. Instead of trying frantically to catch up or to ward off the threat by acquisition, it often makes sense for the firm to come to a collaborative agreement with a company which has greater technical know-how but no ready means of bringing it to the market.

5.6 FOR AND AGAINST COLLABORATION

There are three main arguments for pursuing collaborative involvement with other companies as a preferred means of achieving economies of scale, growth and risk control. These arguments seem to be being rehearsed and tested with increasing frequency as we move towards a Single European Market and new collaborative alliances are formed.

1. Collaboration allows flexibility. Collaborative arrangements can continue, they can lead to acquisition or they can lead to a resumption of independence. They allow particular opportunities for synergy to be exploited and they offer specific solutions to problems such as a gap in a product range or a funding shortage for a research and development project. By contrast, acquisition and piecemeal investment have more sweeping and permanent effects.
2. Collaboration is feasible in markets where it is virtually impossible to envisage acquisition, for example because there are a small number of companies which are definitely not for sale.
3. Collaborative arrangements of the sort we have described enjoy many of the benefits that piecemeal investment has over acquisition. Some of the hard decisions which face management after an acquisition are less likely to arise and there is far less risk from competition law.

There are also effects on areas of performance other than profitability, growth and risk control. Collaboration is less likely than acquisition to strain liquidity and although collaboration generates risks of compromising corporate images and expectations of job satisfaction, these risks are significantly less than for acquisition because the ties are looser. Nonetheless, collaboration is unlikely to succeed between companies with diverse or antagonistic corporate cultures and, in the area of job satisfaction, specific objections to improving profitability through collaboration may be raised.

The job satisfaction of key employees, especially managers, should be considered before deciding on collaboration. Piecemeal investment involves managers in the challenge of building up businesses themselves whilst acquisition involves managers in the challenge of taking over and integrating businesses. Collaboration can, by contrast, be seen as involving a loss of challenge, autonomy and responsibility. Under collaborative arrangements, authority for certain decisions becomes shared with another organisation on which management are dependent and over which they have no direct control. Managers who need to feel "in charge" and who cannot establish a dominant position with their collaborative partners experience a frustration which in itself will adversely affect their own performance and the success of any collaboration.

A final drawback of collaborative arrangements is that they may fall foul of legislation to limit restrictive practices. Where it is understood that a joint venture operation will not compete against the partners carrying on the venture, then that understanding or agreement must be registered and will be subject to review by the Restrictive Practices Court. If the agreement is considered contrary to the public interest, it is declared void. In addition, anti-competitive practices of any sort can be investigated and ultimately stopped by the Director General of Fair Trading.

6.

FINDING A FEASIBLE DEAL

6.1 FROM STRATEGY TO SEARCH

If a management team is in a position to say that they wish to pursue a strategy of acquisition, then the first strategy stage is over and they are ready to move on to the second stage, that of the search. For a would-be management buy-out team the acquisition target is obvious. The next issue is how to approach the seller and see whether a deal can be put together and this is dealt with later in the chapter.

Even for everyone else, the question of what to do next is not as daunting as it seems. Management should not just have decided that they want to buy businesses. They should have decided that they want to buy businesses of a particular type, over a predetermined timescale in order to achieve improvements in certain key areas of performance. A properly formulated acquisition strategy contains the seeds of its own implementation.

6.2 A PROFILE AND A TEAM

The first tasks, before starting the search for an acquisition target, are to draw up an acquisition profile and marshall the resources that will be required during the search process.

The acquisition profile is an outline sketch of the sort of business management wish to buy. Creating the profile involves setting up criteria for the screening of potential acquisition targets. The screening criteria can be vague or specific, positive or negative, but they should always be derived from the acquisition strategy itself. As well as covering industry, size and location, the criteria could relate to trading profitability, the scope for integration with current operations, signs of undervaluation, tax status, growth prospects, riskiness in relation to the existing business, corporate image, depth and quality of management and employee characteristics.

The existence of a formally documented profile means that the task of searching for acquisition targets can be delegated and conducted efficiently. It should also ensure that the strategic reasons for seeking acquisitions are not forgotten in a flash of opportunistic enthusiasm. Nevertheless, a perfect match with a detailed profile normally proves elusive and so some type of scoring system should be used to identify adequate fits.

Apart from finance, the key resources required in the acquisition process are people and it is important that the people who are involved understand each other and work as a team from the outset. Employees should be used wherever possible both on grounds of cost-effectiveness and because of their familiarity with the acquiring business. Employees should nevertheless not assume sole responsibility in technical areas where they are unable to stay up-to-date because of limitations on the experience available within the buying company. For this reason, even the largest organisations use the services of outside consultants in some areas.

The smaller business is likely to rely throughout the acquisition process on its regular professional advisers, notably the solicitor, the accountant and the bank manager. Yet even when a smaller company is looking to buy a business, a reasonably broad involvement of company personnel has its advantages. It helps to make sure that the acquisition process is not unduly centred on a single executive and that consensus and commitment are maintained across the management team. The scope for adopting this approach can be limited by the availability of resources or the confidentiality demands of a potential acquisition.

A drawback of involving employees also arises when they have responsibilities in non-acquisition areas. Implementation of an acquisition strategy can lose impetus or be delayed at critical moments because of the employees' responsibilities for the day-to-day running of the existing business. With external advisers it is usually easier, if only by threat and demand, to ensure continuity of effort and to handle peak requirements.

6.3 THE BROKER METHOD

There are two ways of going about finding a business which satisfies the acquisition profile and which its owners are prepared to sell. You can look amongst businesses which are known to be for sale for those which satisfy the acquisition profile. This we call the "broker method". Alternatively, you can look for all the businesses which satisfy the acquisition profile and then see if the owners are prepared to sell. This course of action we call the "research method".

The broker method involves using a merger broker or market maker of some sort. A variety of organisations, such as corporate finance boutiques, commercial and merchant banks, solicitors, accountants and insolvency practitioners, are actively engaged in trying to sell businesses. They also pool information about businesses which are for sale, for example through The Business Exchange or the Accountants' Business Network, and make appropriate introductions.

Newspapers too can act as market makers. The smaller, property-based business such as a shop, a restaurant or a hotel is usually advertised for sale, for example in "Daltons Weekly", while each Tuesday's Financial Times contains details of businesses for sale, often from receivers.

There are some significant advantages in using the broker method. It provides quick and easy access to businesses which are definitely for sale. Up-to-date and detailed information is readily available and it should indicate quite clearly whether or not a company fits the acquisition profile. Furthermore, by making contact with brokers, a buyer's acquisition interests can be more widely circulated amongst people who are likely to come across or be asked to sell businesses which are of interest.

Nevertheless, there is the disadvantage, where merger brokers are involved, that it is usual for them to be paid a percentage commission on the completion of a deal. Therefore it is possibly in the brokers' short-term interest to underplay the extent of any incompatibility between a would-be buyer and their client. If the negotiations subsequently acquire a momentum of their own, an ill-conceived agreement may result. If this appears to be a problem it makes sense to restrain the influence of the merger broker once an initial introduction has been made by insisting on dealing with the seller.

Another disadvantage of the broker method is that by introducing an element of competition for the target, a broker often achieves a much higher price than in a privately negotiated sale. Finally, except where an active matchmaker is involved, it is only possible to identify owners of businesses who are looking to sell, and whose motives may thereby arouse suspicion. It is more difficult to identify those who might be prepared to sell. The research method avoids this problem.

6.4 THE RESEARCH METHOD

The research method is not just more exhaustive than the broker method, it is also more exhausting. The use of an outside specialist to conduct the search should be considered as this helps to prevent loss of momentum during the research method's three phases: compiling a list of candidates; selecting those candidates which fit the acquisition profile; and determining if the selected candidates might be for sale at a reasonable price.

Only after all three stages are potential acquirers as far down the acquisition track as when they identify a business, from a broker's register, which fits the acquisition profile. Nonetheless, there are considerations which should be weighed against the apparent heavy investment that is required by the research method. These considerations usually lead a business with a well thought-out acquisition strategy to use both search methods.

1. Much of the information required by the research method is already known to management if they are looking to buy a business in their own locality, in their own industry or in a closely related industry.
2. Only by following the research method can buyers really be confident that they will end up with a good deal. The reason is that many owners of businesses who could be persuaded to sell would never go to a broker. Quoted companies, for example, rarely offer themselves for sale through a merger broker although this can occur where they are family-controlled. Many private companies are also not prepared to risk the commercial embarrassment that would follow if it became known that they were for sale.
3. Some people simply do not get round to thinking properly about selling their business unless they are approached by a potential buyer.
4. A thorough search identifies the businesses making up a target industry and highlights the competitive characteristics of that industry. Such information is useful in evaluating acquisition prospects, including those identified through the broker method, and in running a target once an acquisition has been made.

Initially, under the research method the would-be buyer compiles a list of candidates which satisfy the most immediately identifiable and basic criteria of the acquisition profile. It is usually easy to produce a complete list of businesses which meet industry and location criteria. A list can be compiled by scouring the Yellow Pages, published industry surveys, trade and local business publications, exhibition catalogues, commercial directories and electronic online databases. Larger companies and professional advisers may well subscribe to such databases which are maintained by organisations like ICC, Kompass and Jordans.

The second phase of the research method involves collecting sufficient information on each of the businesses shown on the initial list to be able to determine whether they do in fact fit the acquisition profile. As soon as a particular candidate appears unlikely to satisfy the profile then research on that candidate should stop.

6.5 USING ACCOUNTS

Sets of accounts constitute the first major source of information. In the case of candidates which are publicly-held, there are few problems. A quoted company's latest annual accounts are available free on request from the company itself and an Extel card, which can be bought for a small cost or viewed in larger public libraries, shows five years' accounts. In addition, the information available from the company and Extel includes half year trading statements. There are also several directories, such as the Stock Exchange Official Yearbook and the Hambro Company Guide, which provide summarised financial information on all quoted companies.

On the subject of quoted company accounts, the original flotation of a quoted company is marked by the issue of a prospectus. A prospectus normally includes five years' accounts and contains other information relevant to a potential purchaser of shares covering all aspects of an acquisition profile. The usefulness of a prospectus depends on how long ago the company in question first offered its shares to the public.

The accounts of candidates which are privately held or which are subsidiaries of quoted companies present more problems for the researcher. The accounts are only available through Companies House and the accounts filed there may be significantly out of date if the company only just manages to file its annual accounts within ten months of its year-end or if it fails to meet this legal requirement. Less information is disclosed than for a quoted candidate and the company may even have filed the more limited accounts allowed by company legislation.

A "small company" with, typically, turnover of less than £1.4 million and total assets of less than £0.7 million only needs to file a balance sheet at Companies House. A "medium-size company", which would usually have a turnover of less than £5.75 million and total assets of less than £1.4 million, does not need to show turnover and gross margin in its accounts.

Publicly available accounting information becomes even more sparse where the acquisition candidate is not itself a limited company but is just a division of a company. Company law does encourage the presentation of disaggregated information on sales and profits and the requirements of The Stock Exchange for quoted companies are stronger. It still remains unlikely that much numerical information will be available about an individual division.

The best hope of obtaining additional accounting information about a division arises when it is carrying on the activities of a recently acquired business which had to publish accounts. Furthermore, where a business is acquired by a quoted company, the buyer often has to issue a circular to its shareholders which contains much the same information on the acquired business as would appear in a prospectus.

The availability of accounting information is at its worst for businesses which do not have any publication duties imposed on them by law. The most important examples are partnerships and sole traders. The liability of the partners and individuals involved is unlimited and so, in contrast with limited companies, such businesses do not have to publish information for the purpose of protecting creditors.

Before moving on to other sources of information, it is worth pointing out that at Companies House a public or private company has to file not only its accounts but also other documents of potential interest to a buyer. These include a list of directors which shows their other directorships, their addresses and, in the case of public companies, their ages. There are details too about who owns the shares of the company and which lenders have charges over the assets of the company by way of security. Searches of a company's records for accounts and other information can be performed either in person or for a small fee by a number of agencies. Summarised Companies House records are available through several electronic online databases.

6.6 OTHER SOURCES OF INFORMATION

After accounts, the second major source of information is the press. The press can sometimes provide an up-to-date insight into the prospects of an acquisition candidate, its possible undervaluation, its corporate image, its management and its employee relations. The major difficulty of using the press is that it can be very inefficient even if only the relevant local papers or specialist trade press are searched.

Where the target is quoted or is a highly visible private company, it should be possible to use a press cutting service to find out what has been written about that company for a wider audience. The McCarthy Information Service produces sheets of press cuttings on individual companies. These sheets can be bought or, like Extel cards, they can be viewed in larger public libraries. The information is also available on microfiche or on-line and there are other electronic online databases, such as Text-line, World Reporter and Nexis, which carry details of press articles on major companies.

The third major source of information is the candidate's own promotional material. Advertisements, sales catalogues, individual product brochures, price lists, exhibition stands and customer seminars will all provide valuable information on competitiveness, potential for improvement, corporate image, key selling points and the quality of management and employees. Furthermore, the recruiting literature, particularly the graduate recruiting literature of larger organisations, gives insights into corporate image and patterns of advancement and remuneration. Whilst it might take imagination to secure invitations to marketing and recruiting events organised by the candidate and to obtain all price lists, it should be fairly easy to get hold of most forms of promotional literature.

People who have dealt with the candidate are a fourth major source of information. If the would-be buyer is already a supplier, customer or competitor of the candidate, which is often the case, this will serve as a useful starting point. Nevertheless, it is important to ensure that several opinions are sought so as to avoid bias or parochialism. To this end it is useful to sound out, on an informal basis, a number of suppliers and customers. It can also be worthwhile tracing and interviewing ex-employees of the candidate company who work for the potential acquirer.

At a minimum, credit references should be obtained from agencies such as Dun & Bradstreet, Guardian, UAPT and CCN Systems. In this way, the payment experience of the candidates' suppliers, in conjunction with publicly known accounting and legal information, will be accessed.

6.7 MAKING CONTACT WITH THE SELLER

All the types of information source we have discussed do not need to be tapped dry for every acquisition candidate. The search activity should stop once a point is reached where it is obvious that the candidate either does or does not fit the acquisition profile. When a candidate does fit the acquisition profile then it is time for the third and final phase of the research method. This phase involves establishing whether a candidate which fits the profile can be bought. How the potential purchaser determines whether a candidate can be bought depends upon who can actually decide to sell.

A company which is widely held by the public can always be bought at a price. It is advisable to study the company's shareholder profile to identify the sorts of people who would need wooing. Although shareholdings of more than 5 per cent should be disclosed in a quoted company's accounts, some companies themselves have difficulty in identifying the true beneficial owners of significant stakes held by nominees. Nevertheless, consultation with stockbrokers and stock market analysts should indicate the sort of offer which would secure control. People trying to buy public companies normally attempt to speak to the target's directors or advisers prior to making an offer unless it is obvious that such an approach will receive a hostile reception.

Where a candidate is a subsidiary of another company or a division of a company, then the ultimate parent or at least the UK parent company management has to be contacted. Where the potential target is either a private or quoted company with a few dominant shareholders, then the subject needs to be raised with those shareholders. It is not however enough just to identify the right group of people. As part of the research effort, management should also find out who the key decision-maker is in the relevant groups. If there is no key decision-maker or consensus figure, then the acquisition ought to be approached with care because an agreement will be difficult to reach.

Insofar as initial contact is required with management or shareholders then this is most fruitfully arranged through the chief executive or chairman of the possible buyer on some general pretext such as "to discuss matters of mutual benefit". Alternatively, where the interested party wishes to maintain anonymity, a professional adviser can make the first approach. An obvious case in point is when management are thinking of staging a buy-out but do not wish to endanger their careers by making an overt but unwelcome enquiry.

Most attractive businesses receive frequent approaches and so a seasoned seller is unlikely to enter into any serious discussions unless the potential buyer's identity is disclosed. It is however worth seeing if the question of price can be broached as early as possible. A professional intermediary who does not disclose the client's name can ensure that a realistic amount is discussed from the outset.

6.8 IS A DEAL FEASIBLE?

Even if you have made contact with a business which fits the acquisition profile and which appears to be for sale at a reasonable price, you should not go rushing straight into the protracted and costly process of buying it. There are three brief exercises which it makes sense to try and complete beforehand.

1. Meet the key people, namely the sellers and any management you
   need to retain, to establish whether you can work with them during the acquisition and afterwards
2. Draw up an outline of the deal which everyone can accept as the
   basis for detailed negotiation
3. Perform a high-level financial appraisal of the proposed acquisition to identify the expected financial benefits and ensure that
   these are sufficient to justify the capital outlay and the financing
   costs

The three steps are applicable to any type of acquisition, be it an asset
strip, turn round, investment, takeover or merger. The scope for carrying them out is often limited when acquiring a public company but it is
always useful to try because it becomes more and more difficult to extri-
cate yourself from a flawed acquisition once you are committed to real
negotiations and have run up costs. The issues that need to be dealt with
are summarised in Appendix I.4 in our Issues Management Guide.

Meeting the key people helps to address central issues we have met
before, such as the performance of previous management and the
buyer's ability to sort out or integrate the target after acquisition. It also
helps to address two new issues: the possibility of a stalemate; and the
emergence of a serious skeleton in the target's past or some deep-seated
operating problem which will only be admitted in a one-to-one
situation.

Similarly, drawing up an outline of the intended deal highlights the
possibility of stalemated negotiations by flushing out fundamental differences. Also an indication of the assurances which a buyer may seek
from the seller could lead to the early disclosure of show-stopping reve-
lations. It is usually desirable to ensure that any outline agreement is not
binding and does not attempt to duplicate what will be in the full agreement which results from detailed negotiations. In some circumstances it
can be valuable, however, for there to be a binding commitment which
gives a buyer exclusive negotiating rights for a limited period on the
understanding that all information disclosed by the sellers is given in
confidence. Apart from imposing an obligation to negotiate in good
faith, this does not tie the buyer's hands to the deal identified in the outline agreement.

Buyers and sellers are nonetheless sometimes keen to enter into
"heads of agreement" and it is all too easy to find that these are binding.
Consequently, the whole process of buying a business can be short-
circuited and any opportunity to negotiate a better deal is lost. The best
way of ensuring that such heads of agreement are not binding is to make
a statement to that effect in the document or to mark it as "subject to
contract".

A high-level financial appraisal addresses the final key issue we identify. It indicates whether the buyer can realise the strategic purpose of the acquisition while paying the price referred to in an outline agreement. Such an exercise can alert a would-be buyer to the need to sell off some of the target's operations or assets immediately after an acquisition. Consequently, the search for interested parties is begun at an early stage and a rushed or forced sale is avoided. On the basis of the appraisal, a buyer can also start to sound out those who might be expected to finance the acquisition.

If the financial appraisal is not carried out, the buyer may have to backtrack later in the negotiations or drift into foreseeable liquidity problems as a result of the acquisition. If a deal is seen to be feasible, the buyer can pass with confidence from the second stage of the acquisition process, the search, to the third stage of actually "buying a business".

7.

NEGOTIATING THE PURCHASE

7.1 THE BUYING PROCESS

By the buying process we refer to a set of activities which begin once a target and a feasible deal have been identified. These activities come to an end either when some insurmountable problem is encountered and the deal is called off or when a deal has been reached and the acquisition made. The importance and scope of the activities involved vary from deal to deal. They depend in particular upon whether the buyer is a private or quoted company, whether it is proposed to acquire assets, a private company or a quoted company and, in the case of a quoted company purchase, whether the management of the target want the acquisition to go ahead.

The buying process comprises six main activities which are dealt with in Chapters 7 to 18, as indicated below.

1. Negotiation (7)
2. Valuing the business (8)
3. Structuring the acquisition (9, 10, 11, 12)
4. Securing legal protection (13)
5. Investigating the target (14, 15, 16, 17)
6. Protecting the investor when buying in public (18)

Where the target is a quoted company, there is usually limited scope for securing legal protection or for investigating the target. If neither the buyer nor the target is quoted or part of a quoted group, there is no need to comply with regulations for buying in public.

Later on in this chapter, we look at how to prevent stalemate and bring the buying process to an advantageous conclusion by planning properly for negotiations. The aim is to agree on a price and terms which allow you to realise the strategic purpose of an acquisition and secure a net benefit from it. Before then we highlight the issues which the other activities address and we look at how to organise and manage the activities of the buying process.

7.2 VALUING THE BUSINESS

Virtually any issue that arises during the buying process can be dealt with by altering how much you are prepared to pay for the target although this could make your offer unattractive and uncompetitive. For example, you can discount the valuation to reflect doubts about your understanding of the target's business and its previous management or doubts about your own post-acquisition management skills. You can also reflect uncertainty over how the acquisition will affect your existing operations or over any skeletons you suspect that the target has. Nevertheless, valuation is difficult and indeterminate and the requirement to reflect the risks of an acquisition in the valuation can be limited by dealing with some risks in other ways.

The idea of a buyer's valuation is to determine the maximum amount which can be paid for a target. The valuation exercise requires a thorough understanding of the strategic purpose of an acquisition and the formulation of clear plans for post-acquisition management. It also calls for honesty and discipline. It is all too easy to get carried away by the excitement of the acquisition process and convince yourself that the fanciest price is justified.

7.3 STRUCTURING THE ACQUISITION

When you buy a business, you can buy a controlling interest in the shares of a company carrying on the business or the assets used in the business. When the target business is carried on by a partnership or sole trader, rather than a company, then invariably the assets used in the business are bought. The difference between buying shares and buying assets fundamentally affects the risk of an acquisition. When the share capital of a company is bought, the buyer acquires for better or for worse the entire legal and tax history of that company.

The "consideration" that is paid for a business can take the form of cash, shares in the buyer's company, debt or any combination of the three. The object is to finance an acquisition in a cost-effective way and so protect profitability while not exposing the buyer to liquidity problems, high risk and shareholder dissatisfaction about dividends. Questions of what to buy and how to pay do not just have risk and financing implications. They also have profound effects on tax planning and accounting.

The aim of tax planning is to improve the profitability and liquidity of a buyer. It is particularly useful if buyers can make a transaction more attractive to themselves without having to disadvantage the seller. In addition, tax planning can be used to resolve potential stalemates in negotiations. For example, by identifying tax savings for the seller, the buyer can make a deal more attractive to the seller without having to give anything away.

The accounting consequences of different acquisition structures are perhaps surprisingly important. The hazards of forecasting performance and of assessing the net benefits from an acquisition, make it difficult to judge, in an arithmetical sense, whether an acquisition is justified and likely to succeed. This is the challenge of the valuation process. Furthermore, because of the difficulty of unscrambling the effects of an acquisition, it is even hard to assess in retrospect the success of an acquisition and the appropriateness of the price paid.

More relevant in practice is whether an acquisition is seen to be successful. How an acquisition is seen depends significantly on the accounting treatment of the deal which the buyer is obliged to adopt. Despite the technical challenges that are entailed, management should be aware of how acquisitions affect the appearance of their accounts because it is the accounts which are used by outsiders to assess management's performance. The accounting treatment can also have a significant impact on the buyer's ability to pay dividends in the future.

Finally, by planning the accounting treatment of an acquisition, a buyer can secure benefits which cost the seller nothing, so reducing the risk of reaching a stalemate or losing the deal to a rival. Nevertheless, acquisitions made at prices in excess of realistic valuations ought to be avoided irrespective of the accounting treatment that can be adopted.

7.4 MANAGING THE BUYING

After discussing valuation and structuring, we consider how to secure legal protection from the risks of acquisition. Buyers can set conditions for the acquisition and limit the post-acquisition actions of sellers. The target business can be hived down into a new company and assurances and guarantees can be sought in the form of warranties and indemnities. These warranties and indemnities protect the buyer against undisclosed or uncertain aspects of the target's business and can be enforced through retention arrangements.

There is an overriding message of "caveat emptor" or "buyer beware", especially when shares are bought because there are no implied terms to protect a buyer as there are in a contract to purchase goods or services. Uncertainty about the outcome of an acquisition can be limited by investigating the target to understand its industry and its previous management better. An investigation also provides an opportunity to identify problems from the past relating to commitments to employees, legal matters and taxation.

The final activity of the buying process is concerned with the special skills of managing acquisitions with a public profile and ensuring that the deal is not prohibited by regulations to protect investors. Two of our recurring issues are concerned here: making sure that a deal is not stalemated; and seeing that the buyer's corporate image is not tarnished by shoddy treatment of investors.

The challenge involved in managing the buying process is not one of arranging the six activities so that they occur in a single neat sequence. Although all of the activities are interdependent there is no logical sequence. The key point is to ensure that all the activities start soon enough and are pursued with sufficient skill and vigour to be finished in time for the planned completion date.

Management need to manage the timetable for an acquisition. The starting point is a legal completion or public announcement date which makes commercial sense and which sets a limit to the disruption to the buyer and the target which can be caused by acquisition. Deadlines then need to be set for each party and each professional adviser to complete their activities. For public acquisitions, the production of a timetable will be in part dictated by Stock Exchange and Takeover Panel requirements. Nevertheless, even in these circumstances management ought to make sure that the timetable allows them and their advisers to give due consideration and weight to the various activities of the buying process.

If management are to manage the buying process, they need to keep in mind the issues which each buying activity is intended to resolve. Our views, which we present in this and subsequent chapters, are summarised in Appendix I.5 in the Issues Management Guide.

Management do not of course need to be able to carry out all the six activities of the buying process themselves. The activities are too detailed and diverse and even the most sophisticated organisations have some work performed by outside rather than in-house professionals.

7.5 USING PROFESSIONAL ADVISERS

The specialists who can become involved in the buying process include accountants, solicitors, merchant bankers, stockbrokers, public relations specialists, property valuers and actuaries. Prior to the buying stage, a variety of professionals, consultants and brokers may already have been involved in developing an acquisition strategy and finding a business to buy. For the potential buyer who is alarmed at the potential cost of this panoply of experts, it is sensible to broach the subject of fee levels in advance of work being performed and to agree clear instructions about what is required.

It may also be possible to negotiate fees which are in part contingent upon the completion of a deal. Some advisers are prepared to work on a "no deal no fee" basis while others discount the price they charge for their time depending upon the outcome. Such arrangements are useful in ensuring that abortive deals do not have a serious adverse impact on profitability and even liquidity. In management buy-out situations, abortive fees are particularly daunting since they often have to be paid directly by the managers involved out of their post-tax income. Managers should therefore try in advance to persuade the potential sellers to pay professional fees up to a certain amount.

What do the various experts actually do for their fees? The details of their activities are described in detail as we come across them but they are summarised below.

An accounting firm can become involved in searching for a target, valuing and investigating it, giving tax planning advice and reporting on the financial information which the buyer has to present in a public acquisition.

A firm of solicitors conducts legal investigations into the target and draws up the contracts connected with an acquisition. Solicitors can also advise on matters of competition and taxation law and contribute to any public documents which need to be issued.

In private deals, accountants and solicitors often also play the role of co-ordinating adviser and assist in the financing of an acquisition by arranging introductions or presentations to commercial banks.

A merchant bank typically becomes involved in larger public acquisitions and plays a leading role. Merchant banks liaise with the authorities while advising on strategy, search activity, tactics, valuation, timing, financing and public presentation. Furthermore, a merchant bank usually underwrites any cash alternative offered to the target company's shareholders in a public bid.

A stockbroking firm, as well as having an input on broader issues, acts as the essential link in public acquisitions between the buyer, the buyer's shareholders, the target's shareholders and The Stock Exchange. This role is important both in purchasing shares in a public target and in distributing shares issued by a public buyer to finance an acquisition.

Despite a virtual ban on advertising, public relations specialists are useful in contested public bids. Other specialists, for example property valuers and actuaries, are called upon to perform specific exercises connected with an acquisition such as valuing the target's properties or reviewing its pension commitments.

Management do need to have a familiarity with the major issues to be addressed by the experts if they are to be effective in selecting and leading a team of advisers with appropriate credentials, in preventing unnecessary effort and in controlling costs. Moreover, management need to understand how the activities involved in buying a business are connected and how they affect the final judgement as to what is and what is not a worthwhile deal.

As an example, investigating accountants may discover the risk of an underfunded pension liability in a target company. Management need to make sure in the first place that their investigating accountants are looking for such a risk. They should also appreciate the implications of the problem and, as appropriate, consult an actuary, agree terms with the seller to compensate for the risk and have solicitors reflect these changes in any final purchase agreement. This is not however just a matter of understanding the issues, it also requires skilful negotiation.

7.6 THE ROLE OF NEGOTIATION

There are two basic routes to concluding a deal to buy a business. One involves bargaining directly with individuals, while the other involves making an offer to a large number of individuals and trying, from a distance, to persuade them to accept. The latter occurs in highly visible contested bids for public companies.

Nevertheless, all types of acquisition, including public takeovers, require a significant amount of private bargaining. A contested public bid is often preceded by intense private negotiations with the target's management in an attempt to secure agreement. Moreover, public bids involve close discussions with key investors and it is essential that the buyer develops good relationships with institutional shareholders, as well as with financial journalists, long in advance of a public acquisition attempt. Both in private and public acquisitions, negotiations with any investors who are backing a deal can be as intense and important as negotiations with the sellers.

The negotiation skills involved in buying a business are really no different from those required in bargaining to buy anything else in business such as unionised labour or raw materials. Out of all the activities involved in acquisition, negotiation is the one in which management themselves are likely to be the most actively involved and the most experienced.

7.7 WHAT IS ON THE TABLE?

Price is usually the principal item for negotiation with the seller. By way of preparation, the buyer should perform a thorough valuation exercise and define a range of prices within which a sensible deal can be struck.

How the price is to be paid is the next issue. It can be paid in the form of shares in the buyer, debt, cash or any combination of these three possibilities. The price can also be immediate, deferred or contingent upon future results. Tax planning and accounting objectives are frequently of crucial importance in determining an appropriate form of consideration.

What precisely is to be bought is also negotiable. Will it be assets or shares in an established company or a hive-down company? Can the buyer also choose to take over some assets or some operations but not others? Once again, tax planning objectives need to be recognised and worked on during the negotiation to come up with a mutually acceptable deal.

The legal agreements between the buyer and the seller are additional matters for negotiation. They usually include conditional terms and provisions to tie key people in to the target business and restrict the actions of sellers. There are also warranties and indemnities. Although most warranties and indemnities are given by the seller, the seller is likely to seek some undertakings from the buyer and some limits to the scope of any future liabilities. It is normal to restrict both the amounts involved and the timescale for seeking redress.

Receivers however always want to sell without giving any warranties and indemnities because their own knowledge of the business is limited and they do not want any continuing involvement with the buyer. A buyer should not try to change a receiver's approach. Success in that direction is unlikely and, besides, warranties and indemnities from an insolvent company would be worthless. Instead, the buyer should seek to ensure that the consideration reflects the higher risk to the buyer and the terms which the seller wants for completing the disposal.

Receivers want to sell for cash to satisfy debenture holders and secured creditors and they generally want to sell quickly before the business has deteriorated to the extent of being unsaleable. It is not enough to agree a deal in principle with a receiver, you have to deliver the cash before anyone else in order to win.

7.8 NEGOTIATING A BUY-OUT

A management buy-out team can find the process of negotiation rather uncomfortable because they are dealing with the "boss" or the "head office" which has previously had authority over them. They can feel an unwillingness to argue or to ask questions when they think they should know the answers already. One temptation in this situation is to lean more heavily on a professional adviser to act as an intermediary. It is indeed a good idea to have an intermediary make the first approach to see if the target business is for sale, but there are dangers in continuing with this tactic.

The management team has to negotiate not just with the sellers but also with the potential backers of the buy-out. Would-be investors are assessing the prospects of the buy-out largely on the basis of how the managers impress them. However good a management team's plans and financial projections look, it cannot but detract from their credibility if the team appears too deferential and respectful towards their present bosses.

Anyway, the management team should appreciate the strength of their bargaining position and probably only they can play it to its full advantage. The sellers are sometimes under considerable pressure to sell to management. Not only does it make the sellers look socially responsible, but it reduces the need for detailed investigations and the risk of confidential information being disclosed to competitors. In addition, once a management team has expressed an interest, the value of the target to an external buyer can drop considerably because buyers are wary of inheriting a disappointed and unsettled set of managers. Much depends on the uniqueness or otherwise of the management team's skills and experience.

7.9 PLANNING TO NEGOTIATE

Negotiation should be a planned activity if it is to be efficient. Inefficient time spent in negotiation is always costly because it distracts the buyer and target managements from looking after their businesses and it runs up professional fees. Inefficient time spent in negotiation can be even more costly if it sours the relationship between buyer and seller to the extent that a mutually beneficial deal is not concluded. Bitterness can also develop which harms post-acquisition performance.

A major source of inefficiency arises when the seller is dealing concurrently with a number of potential buyers. The seller's intention is sometimes to play off one buyer against another and introduce elements of haste and competitive bidding into negotiations. Buying management do not want to miss a golden opportunity because they cannot react quickly. They can however insist that the seller grants them exclusive negotiating rights for a reasonable period of, for example, six weeks during which they should be able to agree a deal and the related finance.

In order to establish their seriousness and integrity in seeking exclusive negotiations, the buying management should also consider volunteering to enter into a confidentiality agreement with the seller.

A prerequisite for the effective planning of negotiations is that throughout the buying process management should be aware of the factors which affect the final form of the purchase agreement. This awareness comes from monitoring the other five activities we have identified of valuing the business, structuring, securing legal protection, investigating the target and, if relevant, complying with the regulations affecting publicly held companies. Any concerns which have surfaced in these other areas should be brought into the negotiation by the management team without them having to drag a whole host of expensive professional advisers into each meeting.

Against this background, management should plan each meeting or each round of negotiation in a purposeful manner. At the start of any meeting to discuss the terms of an acquisition, both parties should be aware of what has been agreed so far, what is outstanding and what is to be covered in the forthcoming session. It is all too easy to find that the only properly planned meetings are the ones at which exchange of contracts and completion take place and those are meetings which are usually orchestrated by the solicitors acting for the buyer and the seller.

Finally, it is essential when planning for negotiations to define in broad terms the stances that will be adopted. Imagination is needed here and brainstorming sessions before each round of negotiation can be used to consider problems from new angles and to generate new ideas for introduction into a negotiation. For example, tax planning ideas can be used to breathe new life into apparently stale negotiations. Furthermore, it is important to make sure that, in the heat of bargaining, significant points are not conceded while insignificant items are staunchly defended. Therefore, in advance of any negotiation, management should identify priorities, areas of flexibility and tactics.

7.10 NEGOTIATING TACTICS

Although buyers want to secure the best possible deal for themselves, sellers only want to sell if they too think that they have obtained a good deal. After all, they might be selling the results of a lifetime's work. Consequently, in a negotiation you are not trying to beat the seller. You are only trying to beat rival buyers and perhaps alternative options for the seller, such as flotation, by selling yourself and your deal. Even if the seller has no real alternatives, there is little point in trying to win a visible victory. Indeed, the humiliation of a weak seller can be costly in terms of the post-acquisition performance of the target.

If the sellers are to feel that they have secured a good deal, then they, like the buyers, must win some concessions. Accordingly, the preparation for bargaining should be extended to cover planned concessions. It is however important that the opening position adopted by the buyer is credible. No real concession is involved in moving away from an insultingly low offer. It is also wise to make the most of any planned concessions by using them to achieve a notable reduction in tension, thereby making it more likely that the seller will reciprocate.

Buyers should not become obsessed with an issue or entrenched in a particular position and they should avoid defining certain conditions as non-negotiable or certain demands as absolute. This merely leads to confrontation and transforms the negotiation into a contest.

Where sellers are represented by negotiators, it can be beneficial to identify ways of making the negotiators lose sight of the sellers' true interests. This is possible where a target's management are bargaining on behalf of their shareholders. A soft approach can be taken with management on job security, benefits-in-kind, salaries, golden handshakes and so on.

Finally, buying management should try and appreciate what tactics are being used on them. While seeking to understand the opposition, the buyers should recognise that they are probably their own most formidable adversaries. Hard as it may be to accept, there is ultimately no point in agreeing to a bad deal, no matter how much money and energy have been put into the process of buying a business. Managers have to resist the great temptation of trying to save a deal or outbid a rival at all costs. They must instead stick to a range of sensible prices reflecting the value of the target business to them.

8.

VALUATION

8.1 THE USE OF VALUATIONS

When, as a potential buyer, you set about valuing a target business, it is with one purpose only: to establish the highest price at which the acquisition of the target is just worthwhile. The valuation establishes what the target is worth to you as a buyer and so it only makes sense to pay less than that amount. The valuation represents an upper limit price and not a budget for a buyer or a "fair" price on which a buyer and a seller should reasonably agree. We need to introduce two further amounts before we can start to identify ranges of prices over which agreement can be reached.

First, there is the seller's best alternative: this is the maximum value which the seller can derive from the target business either by retaining the business, floating it or selling to somebody else. If the seller's best alternative is higher than your own valuation, then you cannot possibly conclude a sensible deal with the seller. As a consequence, the more buoyant the demand for businesses, the less likely it is that you will be able to clinch a sensible deal with a given seller.

Second, there is the buyer's best alternative: this is the cost for the potential buyer of achieving what the acquisition would achieve by the cheapest alternative means, for example by piecemeal investment. If this is less than the valuation of a target then it may not be sensible to acquire the target even at a price which is below the buyer's valuation.

The table below illustrates the possible relationships between the different values we have identified and the range of sensible prices at which a deal could be concluded.

Buyer's valuation	Seller's best alternative	Buyer's best alternative	Range of sensible deal prices
30	20	10	None
30	10	20	10 to 20
20	10	30	10 to 20
20	30	10	None
10	20	30	None
10	30	20	None

There are practical perils for any potential buyer who does not carry out a proper valuation and recognise that the result represents an upper limit price. It is also tempting for rival buyers to force each other beyond their original limit prices because they do not want to "lose". It is conceivable that the acquisition of a target by a particular rival may have serious adverse consequences on a would-be buyer and so a raising of an original limit price may be justified. Nevertheless, in general, where contestants do not stick to predetermined limit prices, the only sure "winner" is the seller.

Our main concern in the rest of this chapter is to look at how to calculate the buyer's valuation. Nevertheless, it is important to determine the two other values to establish the range, if any, of sensible prices. Determining the buyer's best alternative is relatively straightforward if the buyer has a similar acquisition prospect for which a feasible buying price could be estimated. It is more likely however that the buyer will need to cost out the expenditure required to achieve a similar result through piecemeal investment.

As for the seller's best alternative, this should not be approached too scientifically and rationally. It is no doubt possible to calculate the benefit that a seller or an alternative buyer could actually derive from a target business. It will however be irrelevant because the sellers and alternative buyers themselves will have their own ideas of the value of the target. These values may appear too high or too low but they are the ones that count. You cannot prevent sellers and other buyers from being irrational. As a buyer you can nevertheless make sure that you are not irrational. With this in view, we will start to develop a practical method for determining a buyer's valuation.

8.2 A SUGGESTED VALUATION METHOD

In theory, to be carried out properly, the valuation of a business involves calculating the net present value of all future cashflows associated with that business by using an appropriate discount rate. In practice this is extremely difficult if not impossible to perform for most businesses and it is hard to relate such an exercise to everyday business talk of earnings, book values and historic cost.

Consequently, we will present a valuation model which is rooted in more readily available accounting and market information but which nevertheless recognises to some extent two important concepts from the discounted cashflow ideal. Firstly, cashflows matter and, secondly, you cannot value an acquisition target if you do not know what you are going to do with it afterwards.

Our method involves combining the results of four exercises.

1. Estimating the sustainable earnings arising from the acquisition
2. Putting a capital value on sustainable earnings by applying a multiple
3. Adding the net proceeds of both realising assets and settling liabilities
4. Deducting amounts which need to be invested in the target business

The method needs to be applied in full for all types of acquisition except for an asset strip where only the third element is relevant. After outlining the principles involved, we give a simplified example. We will refer throughout to the valuation of a 100 per cent holding.

The limitations of the model we use need to be appreciated. In particular, a fuller discounted cashflow valuation is appropriate where the timing of earnings and cashflows are significantly different or where sustainable earnings take a considerable time to achieve, for example because they depend on synergy savings.

8.3 ESTIMATING SUSTAINABLE EARNINGS

Prospective buyers first need to identify the current sustainable earnings of the target business or, to be more precise, the sustainable difference between their own earnings with and without the acquisition. The buyers then have to apply an appropriate multiple to these earnings to derive a value for the target business. The multiple should reflect growth prospects and the rates of return required by shareholders and lenders in the light of the riskiness of the target. Consequently, the valuation will reflect the three key objectives of an acquisition, namely profitability, growth and risk control. Both elements of the valuation, the identification of earnings and the derivation of a multiple, are challenging.

Dealing with earnings first, these sometimes have to be derived by the buyer purely from historical information. Alternatively, the buyer, the seller or the target often compile earnings projections. Current sustainable earnings may differ significantly from past earnings for a variety of reasons. There are the anticipated improvements which characterise the turn round, investment, takeover or merger types of acquisition. These benefits will themselves require careful estimation and where there is significant doubt about the buying management's ability to improve performance, a conservative approach should be adopted.

In addition, adjustments to historic performance need to be made where: excessive expenses have been incurred in the past to depress taxable profits; directors' remuneration has been uncommercially high or low; transactions with related parties have been conducted on distorted terms; and the depreciation charge for fixed assets is unrealistically low given the replacement cost of those assets. Past results should also be restated in accordance with the buyer's accounting policies before applying an earnings multiple.

8.4 CHOOSING A MULTIPLE USING PE RATIOS

A multiple is needed to calculate the capital value of a stream of earnings. If a multiple of 5 is applied to current annual earnings of 30, then those earnings have a value of 150. The same example may alternatively be described as showing a current annual return of 20 per cent.

A price earnings or PE ratio is the multiple that is most commonly referred to in the context of quoted companies. The ratio represents the price of a share in a particular company divided by the current annual post-tax earnings attributable to such a share. Therefore a company with a share price of 184 pence, annual post-tax profits of £23 million and 100 million shares in issue, has a PE ratio of 8 or a related annual rate of return of 12.5 per cent.

For quoted companies, PE ratios vary considerably. They are affected by the riskiness of a company's earnings: if a company is perceived as risky then investors will want a higher rate of return to compensate for the risk and the PE ratio will be lower. PE ratios are also affected by growth prospects: if earnings are expected to grow, then investors will be prepared to accept a lower rate of return as calculated by reference to current earnings and so the PE ratio will be higher. In crude terms the required rate of return is reduced by deducting the anticipated growth rate.

Companies in the same industry are subject to common influences which affect the risks and the prospects which they face. Therefore the

PE ratios in an industry tend to bunch together, with the higher ratios going to those companies with the best prospects of growth and the least vulnerability to chance factors.

The PE ratios of quoted companies give an indication of the sort of returns which shareholders expect to earn on specific investments. Consequently, they can be of great use in valuing an acquisition target. The usual starting point is to find the PE ratio of a quoted company which is in a similar industry to the target and which, in the buyer's view, faces similar risks and prospects. In this way the risk and growth aspects of the target should be properly reflected in the multiple.

8.5 THE LIMITS OF PE RATIOS

Even if an apparently appropriate PE ratio can be found, it usually needs to be adjusted. It should probably be adjusted upwards to reflect the premium that will attach to a controlling interest because it is transactions in small parcels of shares which form the basis for determining quoted companies' PE ratios. Recent public takeovers should be studied to estimate the size of this premium. In addition, more information is usually available to the buyer of an unquoted business and the reduced uncertainty indicates that a higher multiple is appropriate.

On the other hand, a large downward adjustment will also be necessary where the shares or business assets to be purchased are less readily marketable than the quoted shares from which the PE ratio is derived or where the target business is less established than a quoted company in the same sector. In private company deals, the net effect is that PE ratios may be discounted by between 30 per cent and 50 per cent. However, for sizeable businesses with the realistic alternative of flotation available to them, smaller discounts would be normal.

Another factor to be borne in mind by quoted companies is that they should be reluctant to apply a higher PE ratio to the target's earnings than the one applied by the market to their own earnings. If a quoted company uses its own shares to buy another business with a higher PE ratio, then the percentage increase in the number of shares in issue will exceed the percentage increase in earnings. Consequently, earnings per share are reduced. Management can sometimes justify this "dilution" to their shareholders. For example, if the target's earnings are of demonstrably higher quality in terms of growth prospects or stability, there is unlikely to be any dilution in the longer term.

The adaptation of quoted companies' PE ratios is not the only method of arriving at a multiple when valuing an acquisition target. Indeed, at times their application can be inappropriate and woolly-minded. The reason for using quoted companies' PE ratios is that they give an indication of the rate of return which public investors expect from a particular type of investment. However, if a particular acquisition is being financed by lenders, shareholders or management with different views of what is an appropriate rate of return from those held by public investors, then the use of PE ratios could be misleading.

Instead of using quoted companies' PE ratios, management can apply a target minimum percentage rate of return which is applicable to all capital projects or they can estimate their cost of capital. The cost of capital can be the cost of the cash, debt or shares used to finance a specific acquisition or it can be an average cost based on the mix of finance used to fund a variety of investments over a period of time. From a percentage rate of return or cost of capital of say 20 per cent, a multiple of five would be calculated in the usual way.

8.6 REALISING ASSETS AND SETTLING LIABILITIES

Having calculated the capital value of the increase in earnings generated by an acquisition, the first and second stages of the valuation process are complete. The third and fourth stages are concerned with adjusting this value to reflect the immediate effects of converting the bundle of assets and liabilities which currently constitutes the target into the bundle of assets and liabilities which is needed to generate the earnings the buyer is anticipating. In the third stage we look at the net cash effect of realising assets and settling liabilities. To the extent that there is a net cash inflow, this should be added to the valuation and to the extent that there is an outflow, this should be deducted from the valuation.

A buyer should take the net assets shown in the target's balance sheet and make two alterations to the total value. Firstly, the buyer should deduct the book value of the fixed assets that the buyer is going to retain beyond the immediate future. This makes sense because the earnings potential of these assets has already been reflected in earlier earnings evaluation stages of the valuation.

Secondly, the fixed assets that are not going to be retained, including any of the buyer's assets which will now be surplus to requirements, should be restated to their realisable amounts as should all other target assets and liabilities which have previously been misreported or not reported at all.

8.7 HIDDEN ASSETS AND LIABILITIES

It is clearly important to check that the target's accounts have been accurately and prudently prepared and reflect all the assets and liabilities arising up to the acquisition date. Two areas which merit attention from the outset, when appraising a private or public company, are pensions and deferred tax.

There can be hidden liabilities or assets in respect of company pension schemes because such liabilities and assets are only starting to appear on balance sheets as companies begin complying with the requirements of the UK Statement of Standard Accounting Practice No. 24. The contributions paid by a target company at any balance sheet date are usually smaller or greater than those necessary to fund the pensions which have been earned up to that date. "Top up" payments to the scheme can be required or, alternatively, the scheme can make repayments to the company or reduce or suspend contributions in the future. Furthermore, where inadequate or excessive pension contributions have been paid in the past, this should be allowed for when calculating sustainable earnings for valuation purposes.

Turning to deferred taxation liabilities, these represent corporation tax which will probably become payable in the future and which is attributable to events that have already happened. For example, suppose a company has depreciated £250,000 of the cost of a £1,000,000 machine through its profit and loss account but has so far been allowed to deduct £600,000 in respect of the machine in determining its taxable profits. In the future, it will charge a further £750,000 of depreciation through the profit and loss account but will only be allowed to deduct £400,000 of this in arriving at future taxable profits. In other words, in future years the company will be taxed on £350,000 of profit which it will not have been making in those years.

What the company often needs to do is to recognise a liability for the tax that will be due on the £350,000 in the future. This represents a tax liability which has been deferred because depreciation, like certain other items of expense and income, is recognised in different periods for accounts and tax purposes. Similar issues are raised by property revaluations, general provisions against stocks and debtors, trading losses, interest income and pension-related assets or liabilities which are recognised in the accounts. In all these areas there are differences between the tax and the accounting treatments.

The buyer of a company needs to be alert to the fact that target company management may not have recognised the full potential liability for deferred taxation in the accounts. There is however an irresistible argument for recognising the full liability if it is intended to carry out an asset strip because the tax is likely to become payable. Even in other circumstances, the buyer's intentions for the target business can mean that the full deferred taxation liability should be recognised and this ought to be brought out in negotiations.

The argument in relation to deferred taxation illustrates a more general point. In arriving at a valuation, book values should be adjusted to reflect the buyer's intentions, and nobody else's. For example, an asset stripper with no intention of continuing the target business will find it more difficult to realise stocks and debtors in full and will be unable to realise the benefits of prepaid expenditure which is being carried forward in the balance sheet. On the other hand, a more aggressive view can be taken by an asset stripper in agreeing liabilities, since there is no need to maintain a good continuing relationship with suppliers.

8.8 ASSESSING INVESTMENT REQUIREMENTS

The fourth and final stage of the valuation process involves looking at the balance sheet which would be left after carrying out all the realisations and settlements allowed for in the third stage and working out the net investment that needs to be made to allow the business to generate the sustainable earnings which we discussed earlier. This net investment should then be allowed for in the valuation by deducting it from the maximum amount that can be paid for the target.

The key elements of this calculation are fixed asset investment, transitional costs and working capital requirements. In order to put realistic numbers to these items, management must clearly have a good understanding of the quality of a target's operations and of what they intend to do with a target.

It is particularly tempting to underestimate transitional costs when setting a maximum price. Costs are likely to be incurred in making people redundant or relocating them, reorganising production facilities and reassuring key customers, suppliers and employees. It is also important to allow for all the costs of acquisition which have not yet been incurred, including professional fees. In calculating these costs, a buyer should appreciate that they might not be allowed as deductible expenditure for corporation tax purposes and it may not be possible to reclaim the VAT that they carry.

On the working capital front, management should fundamentally reassess what they will need to run the target business. Greater power over customers and suppliers and better operating disciplines can reduce working capital needs in turn rounds, takeovers and mergers. Inexperience in the target industry or planned improvements in customer service levels could however mean that more working capital is needed.

8.9 AN EXAMPLE

The four stages of the valuation of a target are illustrated in a hypothetical example of a target which reports pre-tax profits of £950,000 for the year ending on the proposed acquisition date when it has net assets of £2,500,000.

	£'000
Tangible fixed assets	1,900
Current assets - stocks	1,500
- debtors	1,000
	2,500
Current liabilities - bank overdraft	(800)
- creditors	(900)
Net current assets	800
Deferred tax	(200)
Net assets	2,500

1. Estimating earnings

	£'000
Current pre-tax profits	950
Adjustments for:	
Excess directors' remuneration	100
Purchases from a related company at less than market value	(300)
Anticipated additional discounts due to increased buying power	350
Increased depreciation charge to reflect replacement cost of fixed assets	(180)
Overhead reduction on closure of offices	80
	1,000
Taxation at 35 per cent	(350)
Sustainable earnings	650

2.   Choosing a multiple

Average PE ratio of quoted companies in the same sector as the target	10
Discount of 20 per cent	(2)
Multiple, considered adequate in the light of the buyer's own PE ratio of 9	8

3.   Realising assets and settling liabilities

	£'000
Net assets of target	2,500
Adjustments for:	
Book value of fixed assets to be retained	(1,500)
Inadequate reserve for doubtful debts	(20)
Pension fund surplus	400
Surplus, net of tax, on sale of offices with a book value of £400,000	370
Net amount realised from target	1,750

4.   Assessing investment requirements

	£'000
New fixed assets	300
Redundancy and relocation costs, net of tax	500
Investment in working capital	1,100
Professional fees not yet incurred	100
Total investment requirements	2,000

Summary of valuation

		£'000
1.	Sustainable earnings	650
2.	Valuation of earnings using a multiple of 8	5,200
3.	Net amount from realisation of assets and settlement of liabilities	1,750
4.	Investment requirements	(2,000)
Total		4,950

8.10 VALUATION DANGERS

Uncertainty is involved in estimating all four elements of a valuation: earnings, multiple, net realisation proceeds and investment. Consequently, the valuation needs to be constantly updated throughout the buying process as the buyer learns more about the target. Nevertheless, the danger remains that a buyer produces too high a valuation and therefore, using this as an upper limit price, pays too much and so fails to achieve the strategic purpose of an acquisition. Alternatively, a buyer can be so wary of the risks that the valuation and the upper limit price are too low and an excellent opportunity is missed.

The dangers of overoptimism and overpessimism can actually be boiled down to some familiar issues. Do buyers have an adequate understanding of the target industry, the target's management and their own industry? Do they have a realistic view of their own post-acquisition management skills? Are they aware of the target's skeletons?

It is important to appreciate that a buyer can generally seek some recompense from a seller where past earnings have been misleadingly disclosed or where assets and liabilities at the acquisition date have been misstated. The risk in these areas can be passed back to the seller for they were under the seller's control. If however a buyer wrongly estimates the benefits of new ownership on operating performance, chooses the wrong multiple or misunderstands the asset stripping potential of a target or its investment requirements, then there is nobody else to blame. These areas therefore deserve closer attention than many buyers are prepared to devote to them.

There is nevertheless one form of protection which is an exception to the general principle that sellers are accountable for pre-acquisition events only. This option, which is available in the acquisition of private companies, is the earn-out.

An earn-out deal significantly reduces the valuation danger of an acquisition, by linking all or part of the purchase consideration to the post-acquisition profits of the target. As well as addressing valuation risk, an earn-out has the added advantage of easing the initial financing of an acquisition since the target can actually be paid for partly out of cash generated from its own trading. We will look at financing in more detail before returning to the subject of earn-outs.

9.

FINANCING

9.1 THE BASIC STRUCTURE

The basic structure of an acquisition is that the buyer buys the assets of the target business or shares in the company which carries on that business in exchange for shares in the buyer, debts due from the buyer or cash. The flows between the different parties are shown in the following diagram and this basic structure can be applied to acquisitions by the management of an existing business, a management buy-out team or a management buy-in team.

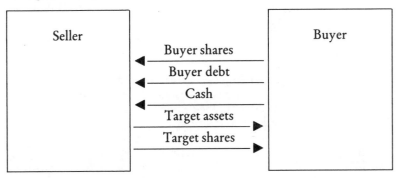

In fact what the buyer needs to finance is not the exact amount which is paid over to the seller as the purchase consideration. This amount should be adjusted upwards for any new investment which the buyer needs to make in the target, and downwards to reflect proceeds from the realisation of any surplus assets which the target may have.

For financing or tax planning reasons a buyer and seller could decide to reduce the purchase consideration by taking assets out of a target prior to sale. Such a move increases, by a corresponding amount, the new investment required after the sale or reduces the amounts subsequently realised from sales of surplus assets. To this end, not only can assets be sold prior to an acquisition, but also dividends can be paid to the selling shareholders or "a purchase of own shares" can take place.

A purchase of own shares can be illustrated quite simply. Suppose a buyer buys 20 of a target company's 100 shares while the target company itself pays out cash to the seller for the remaining 80. The target cancels the shares it has bought and this leaves the other buyer holding all 20 shares in the target. The use of both pre-sale dividends and a purchase of own shares can involve pitfalls. Therefore, although buyers may wish to pursue such options with their professional advisers, we concentrate in this chapter on the core task of paying the seller for all the shares or assets of a business using shares, debt or cash.

9.2 PAYING WITH SHARES

It is appealing to buy a business by issuing shares when the buyer has little cash but has marketable shares which are trading at a good price. Providing the shares on offer are marketable and not too risky, the seller may be happy to accept. Payment by shares is even feasible but extremely rare when the shares in question are not currently marketable but it is intended that the buying company will be floated. Payment by the issue of shares can also be a useful means of securing commitment from a seller who needs to be kept on in the acquired business. If however the buyer's shares are not currently traded, then the recipient is likely to want adequate recompense for the risk of the company not being floated.

Whether or not the shares involved are to be immediately marketable, the directors of a buying company must not exceed the powers to allot shares granted to them either in the company's articles of association or by the shareholders in general meeting.

Managements of listed and USM companies should also be wary of upsetting existing shareholders by not protecting their interests. They can do this by not offering any new shares being issued for cash to existing shareholders and by reducing or "diluting" the earnings attributable to an existing shareholder's shares. This dilution occurs when the purchaser's price earnings ratio is lower than that applied in valuing a target so that the percentage increase in earnings resulting from an acquisition is smaller than the percentage increase in the number of shares in issue.

There are further limits faced by a buyer issuing shares to finance an acquisition, whether they are issued directly to the seller or to an investor. Shares basically confer the right to ownership and participation in profits and so to issue too many shares may lead to undesirable changes in control. In addition, shares carry no assurance that a return will be received or that the outlay will be recovered by the investor. Consequently, investors need to be convinced of the arguments for making an acquisition and the soundness of the buying company's management.

9.3 PAYING WITH DEBT

Included within debt are various forms of bank and institutional borrowing in the form of overdrafts, term loans, leasing finance and so on. For the moment we look at debt as a direct means of payment, as in the case of a loan note or loan stock which is issued by the buying company to the sellers of a business. For borrowers of sufficient stature, a loan note is the simplest form of debt. It can be evidenced merely by a piece of paper and need not be guaranteed or secured. Such a note is usually encashable at specified dates, for example every six months.

When a listed company issues loan stock to the sellers of a business, details of the loan agreement between the company and the stockholders are set out in a trust deed. The stockholders are represented by trustees who negotiate with the buying company on three principal points: security, restrictions and default.

A loan stock can be unsecured, in which case it should be so described at all times, or it can be secured on certain assets of the issuer. Where the loan is not secured, and this may have to be the case where a company has little asset-backing, the trustees usually seek guarantees from individuals, banks or companies related to the issuing company. They are also likely to be more concerned to place restrictions on the activities of the borrower in order to reduce the risk to the stockholders.

Such restrictions usually include restrictions on other borrowings and, in particular, on secured borrowings which rank ahead of the loan stock. Other restrictions can relate to the ability of the borrower to make significant disposals of assets without the trustees' consent, and are aimed at protecting lenders from seeing the substance of the borrower's business disappear. Default conditions are normally also specified under which a loan stock will become instantly repayable. These include failure to make interest or capital payments within some specified grace period from the due date, failure to comply with other terms of the trust deed or failure to satisfy conditions relating to other borrowings.

To the buyer of a business it can appear that debt offers the opportunity to improve earnings per share. Provided the interest cost of the debt is more than covered by the anticipated earnings of the target business, then this must be the case. Nevertheless, debt carries repayment terms and unavoidable interest costs and perhaps also the need to charge assets as security. Consequently, the purchaser's shareholders may see the extra earnings derived from a debt-financed acquisition as no more than compensation for the greater risk they face as a result of the conditions which attach to debt.

9.4 HYBRIDS

Although we have presented debt as a straight alternative to shares, debt can be issued with conversion rights which entitle the holder of the debt to convert that debt into equity on specific future dates at a specified price. Such hybrids of debt and shares can be attractive for both the buyer and the seller of a business.

The seller can benefit from the good performance of the buyer by obtaining cheap shares in the future. However, if things go badly, then the conversion rights will not be exercised and the seller can still have the certainty of a fixed interest debt which has fixed repayment terms and which may be secured. In addition, the issue of a convertible may permit the high past cash earnings of a target's owners to be continued after an acquisition. If ordinary shares were issued immediately, the mainte-nance of the vendors' cash earnings might involve a sudden and signif-icant change in the buyer's dividend policy.

For the buyer of a business, the issue of convertible loan stock can involve a lower interest cost than for non-convertible debt. This is because in exchange for the advantages to a seller of such a stock, a reduction in interest will be acceptable. Nevertheless, best accounting practice recognises that although the cash cost of serving debt may be reduced, any other incentives that are given to debtholders represent costs which should be recorded during the period that the relevant debt is outstanding. The application of this accounting principle could reduce the appeal of such financing.

The issuer of a convertible stock should also be aware of the admi-nistrative costs that will have to be borne. For example, a listed conver-tible stock will be subject to the same regulations as shares. The conversion rights complicate the legal drafting of the trust deed prior to issuing the stock and the exercise of conversion rights has to be monitored.

9.5 FINDING THE CASH

Cash payment has clear attractions for some sellers and they may not be prepared to take anything else. The value of the consideration is certain and the sellers can do what they want with it. Indeed the attractions of cash may constitute a strong bargaining point for a buyer with cash to spend and could lead to a reduction in the amount of the consideration to be paid. Furthermore, a straight cash purchase does not give rise to any continuing obligations between buyer and seller.

There are however costs to the buyer of using cash which do stretch into the future. If the buyer has to borrow to pay cash then there are continuing interest costs. In addition, security may have to be given for such borrowings and the timing of the repayments may not match the anticipated cash resources of the business. Even where the cash is available without having to borrow, an opportunity cost attaches to its use because interest income on the cash balances is foregone.

The three basic sources of cash for a business are shares, debt and profits. Any of these can be used, more or less directly, to finance an acquisition. Whereas profits are generated within the business, issuing shares and taking on debt involve flows with third party investors.

The two sources of cash for buying a business which are shown above are available to any buyer. In favourable market conditions a company may make a rights issue or raise new debt so as to be ready to make cash acquisitions in the future. The third source, namely past profits, is only available to the buyer with an established business and not to a management buy-out or buy-in team. Management teams and also those with small existing businesses who are looking to buy much bigger targets, face significant financing problems. Not only do they lack resources, but they also find it difficult to raise cash.

In these circumstances, the management and the current shareholder base are unlikely to be able to subscribe for significant additional share capital to fund the acquisition. In addition, they do not usually want to see significant amounts of share capital being issued to new investors for fear that their own power will become insignificant and their incentive to succeed will be reduced. Therefore they are forced to raise debt to finance their intended acquisition.

Because the only underlying assets which are available to secure debt are likely to be in the target business, much of the debt may need to be unsecured. The cost of such debt is relatively high and the acquisition will be very risky because a high interest burden makes a business vulnerable if profits dip. We consider the financing of such "leveraged" deals in the next chapter.

In the meantime we consider the conventional financing of acquisitions by existing businesses in more detail. Most managements are likely to set conservative limits on the amounts they raise from debt and their level of gearing or leverage, that is the relationship between debt on the one hand and shares and retained profits on the other.

In addition, all companies face some limit on the amount of shareholders' funds available to them. Private company shareholders will be limited by the private lifestyle they want to enjoy. With quoted companies, there is a limit on the public's appetite for new shares and there are usually minimum levels of dividends which need to be paid out of retained profits.

Consequently, although a buyer may appear to have considerable choice on how to finance a particular deal, there is probably less latitude in choosing how to finance all the buying company's activities in the longer term.

A final point to make on paying in cash is that there is a company law hurdle to clear when a target company gives financial assistance to the buyer for the purchase of the target's own shares. This can occur where the target guarantees or secures any borrowings of the buyer which are used to finance or refinance a purchase of shares for cash. Nonetheless, financial assistance is generally lawful when given by a private company provided that the assistance is properly disclosed and does not harm the target's shareholders or creditors. To demonstrate this, a prescribed statutory declaration has to be made, a specific auditors' report must be obtained and certain special resolutions need to be passed by the target's shareholders.

9.6 DEFERRING THE CONSIDERATION

An additional way of reducing the immediate financing requirement of an acquisition is by agreeing to pay for it on a phased basis. Such arrangements should not necessarily be seen as free financing just because the seller does not earn interest or have some security. The high credit risk borne by the seller is likely to be reflected in a higher purchase consideration. In deciding whether an acquisition is worthwhile, the consideration should be discounted to eliminate the financing element of the price.

When a portion of the consideration is deferred, it becomes easier to pay for an acquisition out of the target's own cash earnings. Nevertheless, if the target's performance is disappointing, then liquidity problems can lie ahead. This is less likely to be the case if the actual deferred payments are contingent upon the future performance of the target as in an earn-out.

Earn-out deals are particularly common in service businesses. The profitability, and hence the value, of such businesses is closely linked to the involvement and motivation of the sellers and the buyer does not have the protection of a high net asset value in the target by comparison with the price paid. The low asset value also limits the ability to borrow in order to pay all the consideration immediately on acquisition.

After an initial payment has been made, further payments are calculated as a multiple of actual post-acquisition profits for a period which may be up to five years. At the end of this period, the target should no longer be dependent on the sellers' involvement if the buyer has succeeded in introducing new management. For a quoted buyer, the multiple that is applied should be lower than the buyer's or else the acquisition could actually reduce the wealth of the buyer's existing shareholders. For this reason, the multiple used to calculate each payment is occasionally linked to the buyer's PE ratio at the time the payment falls due. This helps to mitigate the adverse effect of a Stock Market fall after the original acquisition date. Nevertheless, a buying company with a rising PE ratio may be averse to such an arrangement, and a seller may find it too uncertain.

There are serious potential problems with earn-outs. On a practical level, the management teams of the target and the buyer can become excessively concerned with creative accounting and its detection. The sellers have a clear interest in boosting profitability during the earn-out period, even to the long-run detriment of the business. The sellers will also resent any "interference" from the buyers which depresses earnings in the short-term, even if the interference makes sound strategic sense. Furthermore, even where the rationale for an acquisition involves some element of turn round or synergy, buyers may be reluctant to take measures to improve profitability. They can argue that such measures give the sellers a benefit which they have done nothing to deserve.

To alleviate some of the problems we have described, agreed procedures can be built in to the legal agreements at the time of the acquisition, although such procedures can intensify subsequent wrangling if they encourage a loophole-seeking mentality. Before embarking upon an earn-out deal to ease the financing or reduce the risk of an acquisition, management must think carefully about whether the post-acquisition reality will be bearable and compatible with their strategic objectives.

9.7 ROUNDABOUT TRANSACTIONS

So far in this chapter we have looked at how the buyer can pay the seller in shares, debt or cash. When cash is to be paid over, we have looked at how the cash can be found from the profits of the buying business or from outside investors whether as shareholders or lenders. Yet, many acquisitions by public companies are structured so that outside investors themselves become involved with the sellers. This is done principally to make the accounting treatment of an acquisition more attractive. We consider first the vendor placing, which is an indirect way of paying the seller in cash. We then look at indirect purchases of a target through an intermediary.

The commercial justification for the vendor placing arises when the seller of a business wants cash but it makes sense for the buying company to use paper to make an acquisition either because its paper is highly valued or because cash is not available. The buyer could offer new shares to investors or make a rights issue to existing shareholders and then use the cash raised to buy the target. The vendor placing is an alternative and its principal attraction is that it often allows "merger accounting" and statutory "merger relief" to be applied.

The vendor placing involves issuing shares to the sellers, the "vendors", of the target business. The vendors then have the shares placed by a stockbroker with investing institutions. By selling the shares, the vendors obtain the cash they always wanted. The risks involved in taking the vendor placing route can also be minimised in larger transactions where a merchant bank typically underwrites the placing.

The flows involved in the vendor placing are summarised below.

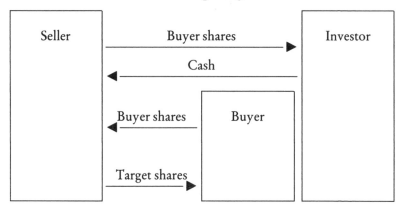

Although the vendor placing is common and widely accepted, it is frowned upon in certain quarters. In particular, it bypasses the statutory pre-emption rights of existing shareholders who, when new shares are issued directly for cash, have the right to subscribe for them in proportion to their existing holdings. The existing shareholders may find that their percentage shareholdings have been reduced and that the vendor placing shares have been issued at a discount on the current market price. A variant which can be used to avoid some of the criticisms of the vendor placing is a "vendor rights issue", under which the vendor's shares are offered to the buyer's existing shareholders by way of a rights offer. Alternatively, the shares may be offered to existing shareholders by way of an open offer under an "open offer and clawback" arrangement.

Turning to indirect purchases of a target through an intermediary, the idea of these has been to avoid the adverse accounting consequences of gradual acquisitions made directly by the buyer. The buyer makes its initial purchases of shares in a target through an intermediary. Subsequently, the buyer can acquire all the shares of the target at once by buying from the friendly intermediary and other shareholders. As a result, a buyer may find that it can secure the perceived advantages of "merger accounting". The flows involved are summarised below.

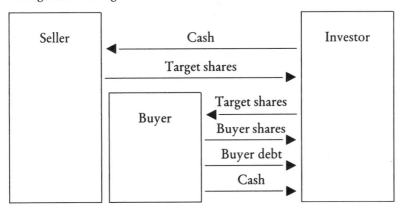

10.

LEVERAGE AND MANAGEMENT BUY-OUTS

10.1 LEVERAGED DEALS

Acquisitions by management teams and acquisitions of large targets by small businesses are often heavily financed by debt and in particular by unsecured or inadequately secured debt.

There is a bias towards debt because it is cheaper than equity and because there are limits on how much equity can be raised, in particular without significantly diminishing the power of the management team or existing shareholders. There is a bias towards unsecured debt because assets which can be used as security are limited and are largely to be found in the target.

Throughout this book we identify matters of particular interest to buy-out and buy-in teams within chapters which deal with the broad spectrum of acquisitions. We believe however that the financing aspects of management buy-outs and buy-ins merit special attention, albeit in a simplified form, because of the special risks that are involved and because a management team is unlikely to be familiar with the issues.

For ease we refer to management buy-outs although most of the material is equally relevant to management buy-ins except where these are carried out by wealthy individuals who have the personal resources to fund an acquisition in full.

10.2 FUNDING BY MANAGEMENT

Two specific financing flows arise when a management team is staging a buy-out. The presentation of these flows is the most straightforward aspect of financing a management buy-out.

Put simply, the buying company in a buy-out or buy-in is an empty shell with no business and no retained profits. The company's first source of finance is the management it is there to serve. Management put in cash in exchange for shares and management are themselves likely to borrow to help fund the purchase of these shares. Often the net cost of such borrowing is very attractive because management can deduct the related interest in computing personal taxable incomes. Our previous diagrams can be extended as follows.

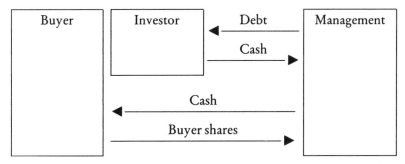

There are of course limits on how much money management can raise and inject in to the company which is set up to buy the target business. The net may be cast wider so as to include other employees for motivational reasons. Nevertheless, even with such additional assistance, in most deals the personal resources of management are likely to be insignificant in relation to the total price of the target.

In fact, if management put up too much of the finance themselves, this could have an adverse effect on the success of an acquisition. Management's main priority is to manage the target business and they are unlikely to do this properly if they are living in fear of personal financial ruin and homelessness. Outside investors usually only wish to see management making a sufficiently large commitment to ensure that failure of the buy-out would hurt them financially. It can also be helpful from the investors' point of view if management take on personal borrowings because this will give an extra incentive to achieve a flotation which will enable them to repay such borrowings. As we shall see, a flotation is often a key objective for a buy-out company in the eyes of outside investors.

10.3 BORROWING FOR BUY-OUTS

If management cannot reasonably subscribe for enough share capital to finance a buy-out or buy-in, what is the next step? The obvious answer is to borrow through the buying company. The immediate challenge in doing this arises because the buying company has no existing business: there are no assets which can be used as security for borrowings and there is no cashflow to help meet debt interest and repayment obligations. It is the assets and cashflow of the target business itself which have to support the borrowings needed to fund a buy-out or buy-in. These borrowings are normally classified as "senior debt" and "mezzanine finance".

Senior debt comprises clearing bank overdraft facilities and other secured borrowings and it is the cheapest form of finance. Secured loans are normally repayable over a period of up to 7 years while overdraft facilities are usually subject to an annual review. The amount of senior debt that can be raised depends principally upon the type and value of the assets that can be used as security. Banks are prepared to advance significant percentages of both the market value of land and buildings and the book value of trade debtors. Funds may also be made available by charges on plant and machinery and stocks although the amounts involved are likely to be small in relation to the assets' book values because what matters to a bank is how much the assets would fetch in a forced sale.

Alternatively, and in larger transactions, banks may be willing to make advances on the basis of a strong and predictable cashflow. Other sources of senior debt include factoring or invoice discounting which can be more efficient than bank overdraft borrowing as a means of raising the maximum amount of finance from fluctuating levels of trade debtors. In addition, leasing and hire purchase can be used to finance expenditure on fixed assets.

It is important when dealing with senior lenders to realise that they are most interested in how badly things might go. There is little point in trying to dispel this concern by emphasising how superbly the buy-out might work, because senior lenders share only in failure, not success.

Mezzanine finance is so called because it lies between senior debt and equity. It is unsecured or inadequately secured lending and it is provided by merchant banks, venture capitalists, other specialist financial institutions and even, perhaps, the corporate seller of a business.

Mezzanine finance is riskier and therefore more expensive than senior debt and the amount that a buy-out can accommodate is limited by the profits that are likely to be left after senior debt interest has been paid. Lenders need to ensure that their interest is adequately covered by available profits. Mezzanine finance normally takes the form of loans repayable over a period of five to ten years, although repayment patterns can be varied to match the projected cashflow of the target. Deferred repayment terms may be attractive to a management team but they increase the risk to the lender and hence the cost to the borrower.

Nevertheless, when repayments are made ahead of an agreed schedule, early repayment penalties may be applied to compensate lenders for their loss of interest income.

The cost of mezzanine finance to a borrower need not just include the running interest cost. There may also be a discount. For example, where a company issues a £100 bond at a discount of £10, it receives £90 but later has to pay the bondholder £100 on redemption. An additional cost is involved if lending institutions are given access to cheap equity by being issued with warrants to subscribe for shares on favourable terms prior to the buy-out company being sold or floated. Under best accounting practice, the full cost of any finance should be recorded in the profit and loss account throughout the period that the debt is outstanding.

The aim of all lenders is to build up a total return which is seen as adequate compensation for the risk of their lending. To the extent though that management establish their credibility and creditworthiness, the risk must diminish. Consequently, management may try to negotiate reductions in interest rates on the achievement of projected profits.

10.4 MANAGEMENT AND OUTSIDE SHAREHOLDERS

If management's own resources and the buying company's borrowings are inadequate to fund an acquisition, then management have to raise additional equity finance. Indeed they may seek to raise such finance even before they have exhausted all borrowing possibilities, if they become nervous about becoming too highly geared. Outside equity finance is expensive because providers see it as risky. Indeed it is a cruel feature of buy-outs and buy-ins that the overall cost of finance can start to rise very quickly as the price goes up and this can put management in a weak position if competitive bidding gets underway.

Institutional shareholders usually seek some ongoing return by way of fixed dividends on preference shares or profit-related dividends on ordinary shares. However, when they put money into a company to help finance an acquisition, institutional investors plan to make most of their return from the capital value of their shares. This value may be realised through a "purchase of own shares", with the buy-out company buying shares back off investors. It is however more usual for the realisation to be achieved through the sale or flotation of the company. Each of these options is referred to as an "exit route".

For a given initial injection of cash, an institution will set a target value for the shares which it will acquire in return. Suppose that this target value is £4.8 million. Further suppose that the business is projected to make profits after continuing senior and mezzanine debt costs and tax of £0.4 million in the year of flotation and that a PE ratio of 10 is considered appropriate for the business. In this case the institution cannot invest since all the shares in the company will only be worth £4 million and so nobody can have £4.8 million of shares.

To continue our example, even if the company was going to be worth £5 million in a situation where the management was putting in an initial investment of £0.2 million, the deal could not go ahead. Management would end up with a derisory 4 per cent stake in the company and no return on their investment. They would not be sufficiently motivated by this to make the acquisition a success.

It is on such fundamental points of commercial arithmetic that a possible buy-out or buy-in may collapse. Unless the situation is totally hopeless, it could be saved by reducing the total price of the acquisition, reducing the cost of borrowing, persuading institutional investors to accept a lower return or by carrying out a credible reassessment of the likely value of the business on a subsequent sale or flotation. In addition, at the cost of increasing the risk involved, management could try and increase their own borrowing and the company's.

Any of the measures we have described improve management's prospective return even where a deal is not about to collapse and they should be the subject of vigorous negotiation. Nevertheless, the relationship between management and their financial backers is delicate and is characterised by mutual dependence.

10.5 WORKING THROUGH THE NUMBERS

To illustrate the logic involved in deciding whether a buy-out is feasible, we will present a highly simplified example. The ratios applied in calculating security requirements and interest cover are hypothetical. The level of gearing shown is purely illustrative and the rates of return are not intended to reflect the actual rates that need to be paid in practice. The rates of return sought by investors depend on many factors: the current interest cost of low risk finance, the minimum lending rate; the riskiness of the business; the strength of management; the degree of asset-backing; the quality of the product range; and the uniqueness of a company's ingredients for success.

Any management team ought to consult, at the earliest opportunity, professional advisers with experience in appraising the financing of a buy-out. It must be appreciated that in real life the calculations outlined below will be plagued by additional complexity and uncertainty. In particular, the valuation of a company on flotation or sale depends on future performance of the business and the state of the Stock Market. In performing any calculations on buy-out financing it is essential to carry out "sensitivity analysis" to see what happens in different sets of circumstances.

The relative stakes in the company which the management and the institutional investors are entitled to immediately prior to a flotation or sale are often governed by "ratchet" arrangements. Usually, under a ratchet arrangement, the higher the profits of the company or its total valuation, the higher is management's stake. Consequently, in assessing whether a buy-out looks attractive, management have to consider the relative likelihood of a wide range of possible rates of return which they might earn.

10.6 A HYPOTHETICAL BUY-OUT

In our example we take a business which costs £4,700,000 and which, although it has no additional working capital requirements, needs £500,000 of immediate investment in new plant and machinery. It is estimated that four years after the buy-out, when investors expect to see the company float, operating profits before interest, but after allowing for taxation of those profits, will be £1,000,000. The feasibility of financing such a buy-out might be approached in six stages.

1. Senior debt

    Management and their advisers estimate that the following debt might be raised at an annual net of tax cost of 10 per cent.

	£'000
Leasing of new plant and machinery	500
Factoring of debtors of £1,350,000	1,050
Overdraft secured on land and buildings valued at £1,000,000	750
Additional overdraft based on cashflow	500
Total senior debt	2,800

    In practice it may be difficult to raise the additional overdraft and such a facility might also be viewed as part of the mezzanine finance package.

2. Mezzanine finance

It is thought that mezzanine finance might be forthcoming at an annual cost of 20 per cent provided that interest is twice covered by profits after senior debt costs. For simplicity, it is assumed that the provider of mezzanine finance does not seek any equity in the target.

	£'000
Profits before senior debt costs	1,000
Cost of senior debt of £2,800,000 at 10 per cent per annum	(280)
Profits available for mezzanine interest	720
Maximum mezzanine interest cost which can be twice covered	360
Maximum mezzanine debt based on 20 per cent annual cost	1,800

3. Funding shortfall

Management can raise personal resources of £100,000 and so calculate the funding shortfall to be made good by an institutional equity investor in the following way.

	£'000
Total cost	5,200
Senior debt	(2,800)
Mezzanine finance	(1,800)
Management equity	(100)
Funding shortfall	500

4. Valuation on flotation or sale

It is estimated that the business could be floated after four years on a PE ratio of 9. Consequently, the value of the company at that time is calculated as follows.

	£'000
Profits before interest	1,000
Senior debt cost	(280)
Mezzanine finance cost	(360)
Profits attributable to equity shareholders	360

	£'000
Value of equity based on a PE ratio of 9	3,240

The above calculation assumes that the senior and mezzanine debt remains in place after the flotation. When, as is usual, some debt is paid off on flotation, the interest on that debt should not be deducted in arriving at the profits attributable to equity shareholders. The value of the equity which is subsequently calculated should however be reduced by the amount of the debt to be repaid.

5. Return on institutional equity

It is estimated that an institutional equity investor might seek an annual rate of return of 50 per cent. Calculated on a compound basis this means that the shares owned by the investor which cost £500,000 should be worth £2,531,000 at the end of four years.

6. Management reward

Finally, the value of management's shares after four years is calculated.

	£'000	Per cent
Total value of company	3,240	100
Value of institutional equity	(2,531)	(78)
Value of management equity	709	22

This calculation means that management receive some 22 per cent of the company and that their initial investment of £100,000 grows at an annual compound rate of approximately 63 per cent to be worth £709,000 after four years. Management need to decide whether this reward is worth the risk and the hard work that will be involved and whether they want to proceed with the buy-out.

10.7 SELECTING INSTITUTIONAL INVESTORS

Before making contact with potential investors, a management team should seek the assistance of professional advisers, such as accountants, with relevant experience. They can help: in seeing if the financing of the deal is feasible; in negotiating senior debt with banks and leasing and factoring companies; in selecting the venture capitalists and other institutions to approach for mezzanine and equity finance; and in preparing a proposal to raise finance for presentation to the institutions.

The proposal document usually contains a full set of financial projections for the first five years and a narrative setting out what management intend to do with the target business. This document must be well thought-out because it will give potential investors an indication of both the quality of the management they are being asked to back and the value of the target business on a subsequent sale or flotation.

The offers received in response to the proposal require detailed evaluation before a selection can be made. It is easy to become confused by conditions, shares with complex names and other jargon, but there are a few questions which are really important.

On the basis of projected earnings, what stakes in the company do management and the institution secure and what rates of return do they earn?

Under the proposed ratchet arrangements, what are the stakes and returns of management and the institution at different levels of earnings?

Do management feel that the institution will be good to work with, reasonable in its monitoring requirements and supportive of the business?

Under what circumstances, as set out in drafts of a share subscription agreement and the company's articles of association, would the institution force management's hand, for example by pushing for a sale or flotation or by insisting that the business be run for cash and not long-term growth?

11

TAX PLANNING

11.1 THE ROLE OF TAX PLANNING

Tax saving is not itself a justification for acquisition. Firstly, tax-driven acquisitions are rarely going to make commercial sense. When a business is sought for its tax benefits, the asking price is likely to rise to reflect a large proportion of the tax benefits to the purchaser. Even where there is still a significant net benefit, this may not fully compensate for the costs and risks involved in searching for, investigating, acquiring and managing the target company. Secondly, tax-driven acquisitions may fall foul of continuing statutory and judicial moves to tighten up on tax avoidance. Care is required even when a commercially justified acquisition is being structured so as to reduce or defer tax liabilities.

Uncertainty as to the possible Inland Revenue approach to aspects of an acquisition can seriously affect the terms on which both the buyer and the seller are prepared to settle. Indeed, the risks might make an agreement impossible. In some circumstances clearance procedures exist which allow the parties to a proposed acquisition to obtain a statement of intent from the Inland Revenue as to how they will view a particular transaction.

Clearances are the province of the tax specialist and are described by reference to the source section numbers of the relevant taxes acts. For example, a clearance under Section 88 of the Capital Gains Tax Act of 1979 covers the ability of sellers to defer their capital gains tax liability when they exchange shares in their own company for shares or other securities in the buying company. A clearance under Section 707 of the Income and Corporation Taxes Act of 1988 covers the Inland Revenue's powers to cancel tax advantages arising out of share transactions. There are other clearances (and section numbers) covering, amongst other things, transactions in land, company amalgamations, demergers and purchases by a company of its own shares.

Initially tax planning for the buyer simply involves understanding the tax consequences of making an acquisition in one way rather than another. This understanding should then be used to the advantage of the buyer to choose an appropriate structure for the deal and to ensure that the final consideration reflects, as far as possible, the buyer's tax costs but not benefits and the seller's tax benefits but not costs.

As we have seen, there are numerous ways of structuring an acquisition: shares or assets may be bought, and cash, shares or debt may be given in exchange. Each different way of making an acquisition gives rise to different tax costs and benefits to buyer and seller.

11.2 BUYING A COMPANY

The first thing to do is to sketch the straightforward tax consequences of buying a company by buying all or substantially all of a target company's shares.

The transaction will not be subject to VAT. It will however attract stamp duty payable by the purchaser at a rate of half of one per cent on the consideration. Moving on to corporation tax, the shares which the buyer acquires do not generate any current deductions in arriving at the buyer's taxable profits. This contrasts with the direct purchase of, for example, fixed assets which give rise to deductions through capital allowances (tax depreciation). The buyer will also not be able to defer the tax due on chargeable gains arising on other capital transactions in the period by deducting them from the base cost of any shares acquired. By contrast, asset purchases, can be used to defer or "roll over" a liability to corporation tax on such chargeable gains.

However, the disadvantages of buying a company should be weighed against the favourable tax opportunities that the acquisition of a company offers. In its past, a target company may have incurred net losses for tax purposes either from trading or from capital transactions. A buyer can in certain circumstances offset these losses against the trading profits and chargeable gains of a successful business after an acquisition.

Also, where a company has paid dividends to shareholders, it will have paid over advance corporation tax (ACT) to the Inland Revenue. The amount of such advance payments can be deducted from the tax due on a company's profits, its so-called mainstream corporation tax. However, a target company which has not made sufficient profits to pay mainstream corporation tax could well have paid out ACT without having received any benefit. It may be possible after an acquisition to offset such "unrelieved ACT" against the tax due on the results of a profitable operation.

We now consider in more detail how the tax legislation can provide some of the benefits we have just described. The question of trading losses is pursued first, to be followed by capital losses and ACT.

11.3 LOSSES AND UNRELIEVED ACT

It is essential to realise that a target's pre-acquisition trading losses cannot be offset against profits in the acquiring company or another member of the same group. The target's pre-acquisition losses can only be offset against the target's own post-acquisition taxable trading profits.

A buyer cannot readily get around the restrictions by transferring profitable operations into the target company. The target itself cannot use its losses if there is a major change in the nature or conduct of its trade in the three years before or the three years after it is acquired. Losses similarly become useless to the target if a trade which has become small or negligible is revived after a change in ownership.

A conflict can arise when a company is bought with the intention of turning it round. The very process of turning the company round can result in such large changes to the way its trade is carried on that past tax losses are put at risk. Consequently, depending upon the buyer's future plans for the target business, the benefit of tax losses may have to be ignored completely when determining the consideration.

Capital losses present fewer problems than trading losses. Whilst they can only be used for offset against chargeable gains in the same company, nonetheless in some circumstances the target's capital losses can be used to offset chargeable gains which would otherwise have occurred in the acquiring company or another group company. This is made possible by so-called Section 273 relief under which chargeable gains are deemed not to arise when assets are transferred within "a capital gains group" where each company is at least 75 per cent owned by its immediate parent and other conditions are satisfied.

In principle, to make use of a target's capital losses, a group can transfer into the acquired target any assets which it may be selling at a profit outside the group in the future. In this way all chargeable gains occur in the acquired company and can be offset against its capital losses. Such a use of capital losses might be refused because it smacks of tax avoidance. However, an official statement from the Inland Revenue suggests that this would only occur where a target was bought primarily for its capital losses. Buyers might still discount the value of a target company's capital losses to reflect some uncertainty as to their use.

In respect of unrelieved ACT, the rules are very similar to certain of the rules on trading losses. Unrelieved ACT in a target company can be offset against its future mainstream tax liability subject to there being no major changes in its business. Once again, a cautious turn round is required.

Unrelieved ACT can also feature in an acquisition in a different way. A company which itself has unrelieved ACT may see a tax advantage in buying a business with a recurring mainstream corporation tax liability. Such a buyer should not necessarily be thought of as a poor performer. It might be that most of a successful UK company's profits are earned and taxed abroad so that the domestic mainstream corporation tax liability is small.

In the case of an assets purchase, the pre-acquisition unrelieved ACT of the buying company can be carried forward and offset against future liabilities for mainstream corporation tax arising from the acquired business. In the case of a share purchase, the buying company could surrender downwards to the acquired company unrelieved ACT arising subsequent to the acquisition of that company.

11.4 BUYING ASSETS

Having now completed our review of the principal possible effects on the purchaser of buying a company, we move on to consider the alternative of the asset purchase.

Whilst a share purchase is definitely not subject to VAT, an asset purchase may be unless an entire business is bought as a going concern to be carried on by the buyer. The acquisitions considered by us are usually not subject to VAT, but if they are, buyers need to be alert to any cash flow advantage for the seller and any disadvantage to themselves.

Stamp duty is payable by the purchaser on the value of those assets which cannot be transferred by "delivery". Such assets include debtors, goodwill, land and buildings. In order to reduce the stamp duty liability, cash and debtors are often not acquired. Therefore, it might appear that the burden of stamp duty is smaller for an asset purchase than for a share purchase because in the asset purchase not all of the underlying assets of the target business give rise to a liability. However, this view ignores the fact that, while in an asset purchase stamp duty is levied on asset values, in a share purchase it is levied on share values which reflect the target's assets net of liabilities.

Where there is a real choice between shares and assets, the purchaser should compare the stamp duty implications and ensure that any additional costs are allowed for when assessing the consideration. Alternatively, a buyer can decide that stamp duty at a rate of half of one per cent is simply insignificant and not worth further analysis.

On the corporation tax front, the purchase of assets has one clear advantage where the consideration paid is properly attributable to fixed assets other than goodwill, like plant and machinery, industrial buildings and even patents, know-how and scientific research. Such assets generate capital allowances which the buyer can deduct before arriving at taxable profits. Where shares in a company are acquired, the shares attract no allowances and the tax history of the fixed assets of the acquired company remains undisturbed. These fixed assets could have negligible values for tax purposes so that few capital allowances will be generated. The allowances that are generated also arise only in the acquired company, not the buyer. The capital allowance disadvantages of a purchase of shares rather than assets should be quantified and allowed for in the valuation of a target business.

There is an additional potential advantage in an asset purchase. The fair value attributed to stock in an asset purchase is often calculated at selling price net of selling costs. However, in a target company's accounts, stock values will be stated at the lower of cost and net realisable value. Since opening stock values are deducted in arriving at profits, lower taxable profits could be reported after an asset purchase than after a share purchase.

So far we have looked at matters entirely from the point of view of the buyer and have highlighted the costs and benefits to the buyer when either the shares or assets route is being followed. Yet what are the factors that are going to influence the seller's wishes about what is sold and what arguments can be brought to bear by a buyer?

11.5 THE SELLER'S PERSPECTIVE

There is a presumption that, given the choice, a seller always prefers to sell shares rather than assets. In the first place, by selling a company, the seller disposes of all the legal problems and tax skeletons that might attach to a company. Furthermore, the seller might only be able to derive value from past tax losses by selling the company. A sale of assets might lead to a running down, alteration or cessation of the trade generating the losses. Such an occurrence would mean that the selling company would be unable to use the losses in future. Nevertheless, judicious asset sales normally generate profits which can enable trading losses to be used.

Without doubt, the most frequently cited reason for a seller preferring a share sale to an asset sale is the "double taxation argument".

Because of its popularity and apparent persuasiveness it merits closer inspection.

An individual selling shares faces a single tax liability for the capital gains on those shares. Similarly, a corporate seller is liable for corporation tax on the chargeable gain arising on a share disposal. There is single taxation of the share sale. There is however seen to be double taxation of the sale in the case of an asset-based deal.

Choosing fixed assets as our example, the first slice of taxation is taken when the selling company becomes liable to corporation tax on the disposal. Insofar as a fixed asset is sold for more than its tax depreciated value, then there is corporation tax on the reversal of past tax depreciation. There is also corporation tax on any chargeable gain that arises when there is an excess of sales proceeds over the original cost of the fixed asset. By way of illustration, suppose that an asset costing £60,000 which had been fully written down for tax purposes was sold for £100,000. There would be corporation tax on the reversal of the previous tax depreciation of £60,000 and corporation tax on the chargeable gain of £40,000.

The second slice of taxation is taken when the shareholders of the selling company try to realise their investment in that company. For example, if the selling company is wound up there will be a disposal of the shares of the company at that date. Accordingly, the shareholder is faced with a further tax liability on any resulting capital gain.

The double taxation argument can be powerful. If a £10,000 capital gain is taxed once at 35 per cent, the net gain is £6,500. If the £6,500 is taxed again at 40 per cent, the net gain is reduced to £3,900. The tax may however be materially reduced because, in computing taxable gains, original pre-March 1982 costs are "rebased" to March 1982 values and subsequent inflationary increases in value are allowed for through indexation. Furthermore, following recent reductions in top rates of income tax, the tax cost of realising sales proceeds can be reduced when an individual receives dividends from the selling company.

The double taxation argument is unlikely to be relevant where the target business is carried on by a subsidiary of another company. The subsidiary can sell assets and suffer taxation on the gains but can then pay up the proceeds to its parent company by way of dividend. Such dividends are not taxable in the parent and are not subject to ACT where the subsidiary is more than 50 per cent owned and both the subsidiary and the parent have filed a "group income election" with the Inland Revenue.

We close our review of the seller's tax position by pointing out that, in a negotiation, the buyer could make considerable play out of being able to identify an opportunity which the sellers and their advisers have missed. For example, a disposal occurs for capital gains purposes when contracts are exchanged and the disposal is unconditional. A buyer may be able to defer a transaction at no personal cost so that a gain is taxed in a later tax year so far as the seller is concerned.

Alternatively, whenever a share or asset purchase from a corporate seller is being considered, the buyer should ensure that the seller is proposing to make the sale from the right company from a chargeable gains standpoint. It might be that the effective proceeds of a sale to the seller can be increased by making sure that the sale is made by a company with capital losses which can be used to offset the chargeable gains on a share or asset sale. To achieve this, assets may have to be transferred within a selling group or the ownership of shares within a group may have to be restructured.

Having considered the tax effects of buying shares or assets, we now move on to look at the tax consequences of funding an acquisition.

11.6 ISSUING SHARES

There is a major potential tax advantage which an issue of shares has over a cash payment. It is the ability to use the relief under Section 85 of the Capital Gains Tax Act 1979. This relief allows corporate or individual sellers to defer the liability for capital gains tax (CGT) on their gains on disposal until the consideration shares are themselves sold. Indeed, where the consideration shares are readily marketable, individual sellers may be able to sell with a minimum CGT liability. If they dispose of the shares gradually over a number of years, they will be able to take maximum advantage of their annual CGT exemptions.

To qualify for Section 85 relief, the consideration shares must be issued as part of a general offer to the target company's shareholders or else the purchaser must end up owning at least 25 per cent of the target's equity. The disposal must also be effected in good faith for commercial reasons and not to avoid tax. A procedure exists under which it can be ascertained in advance of a share exchange whether the Inland Revenue will allow Section 85 relief. This is known as a Section 88 clearance.

In summary, there is a major CGT advantage to a seller who is given marketable shares as opposed to cash. The buyer should seek to reflect this benefit to the seller in the amount of the consideration and should also consider obtaining recompense for any costs incurred in issuing the consideration shares. For example, the buying company can incur considerable professional fees and it receives no tax allowances for the continuing costs of financing the acquisition by a share issue. Interest payments on debt are normally allowed as a deduction in arriving at taxable profits. By contrast, dividends paid to shareholders are never allowed as a deduction in calculating taxable profits.

11.7 TAKING ON DEBT

An issue of debt can, like a share issue, still attract Section 85 relief so that the seller's CGT liability on a sale of shares may be deferred. A secured or unsecured debenture will normally qualify for the relief, although this is an area requiring careful attention.

The receipt of a debt qualifying for Section 85 relief can be especially attractive for a seller when compared with cash. Interest is received on the full gross value of the debt and not on the amount net of CGT that would be received if payment was made in cash. In addition, the benefits of indexation relief and annual CGT exemptions can significantly reduce the CGT cost of disposing of the debenture.

As we have seen, the continuing costs of servicing debt and shares have different tax consequences. Interest costs are generally allowable deductions for tax purposes whereas dividends are not. In the hands of the seller of a business, interest income and dividends are both received with the same rate of tax credit and, for individuals, are taxed in the same way. For a corporate seller, interest income but not dividend income would be taxable.

In structuring an acquisition and comparing interest and dividend costs net of their tax effects, buyers should take into account their own particular circumstances. For example, interest deductions are of no immediate use to a company with tax losses. Meanwhile, the ACT on a dividend represents a real cost, not just a cash flow disadvantage, for a company with a mainstream corporation tax liability which is smaller than the advance payments of corporation tax which it is making by way of ACT.

A rare and risky way for a buyer to mitigate the net of tax costs of debt is to use "deep discount securities". The expert advice of bankers and tax advisers should however be sought before taking any action. Deep discount securities are secured loan stocks which are issued at a price which represents a significant discount on their redemption value. Because a significant cost is borne by the borrower in the form of the discount, the interest cost is low. The interest cost disappears altogether in the case of a zero coupon bond.

A security which is structured in this way is highly tax efficient for the borrower and the lender. For the borrower, any small interest cost attaching to the bond is deductible in arriving at taxable profits when it is paid. By contrast, the heavy discount cost is deductible on an accruals basis and not when it is "paid" on redemption of the security. For the seller, the discount represents income which is taxed on redemption and not on an accruals basis.

The discount cost accruing during a particular period is basically calculated by assuming that the issue price grows at a constant compound percentage in order to reach the redemption price. By way of example, this percentage, known as the yield to maturity, would be 10 per cent per annum on a security issued at £100 and redeemed at £121 after two years.

11.8 PAYING IN CASH

On the capital gains front, an individual or company selling shares for cash cannot defer the taxation liability on the related gains by use of Section 85 relief. Individual sellers of shares must look instead to other forms of CGT relief, such as retirement relief. A seller could also try to time the disposal to use capital losses derived from other transactions or to utilise any unused annual exemption from CGT liabilities.

Where a corporate seller cannot rely on Section 85 relief to defer the corporation tax liability on a chargeable gain, there are a number of possibilities. Current trading losses can be offset against the gain as can brought forward and current capital losses. In the case of a group selling shares in a subsidiary or assets, thought should be given to making an initial transfer of the shares or assets into a group company which has capital losses, prior to the sale.

Another possibility available to the corporate seller is the dividend strip. This involves reducing the proceeds to be derived from the sale by payment of a pre-disposal dividend. However, pre-disposal dividends should not be paid out of artificially created reserves and it is wise to take specific professional advice so as not to fall foul of anti-avoidance legislation in this area. Furthermore, whilst a pre-sale dividend can reduce a gain, it would generally not produce or augment an allowable capital loss. Payment by the target for group relief and surrendered ACT can also have the effect of reducing the target's pre-sale value although care should be taken to ensure that any value-reducing transactions have a proper commercial basis.

Where a company pays cash, the cost of that cash, either in terms of interest charges incurred or interest income foregone, should be thought of net of tax. Interest income is subject to corporation tax and interest charges are generally deductible in arriving at taxable profits.

However, unless the buying company finances an acquisition on an overdraft, interest charges will probably only be allowable as deductions in the period when they are paid as opposed to when they fall due for payment.

When an individual is buying a business, interest income foregone should usually be thought of net of an income tax charge. However, interest charges should not be thought of net of a related tax credit unless the buyer can take advantage of specific tax reliefs that are available. An important case of relief arises when an individual buyer is borrowing to acquire shares in a close company. Although the rules are complex, close companies include nearly all private companies. Individual buyers can deduct such interest costs in arriving at their taxable income subject to satisfying various conditions. This relief is of particular relevance to members of management buy-out teams.

11.9 DEFERRED AND CONTINGENT PAYMENTS

A major commercial justification for buyers in seeking to defer payment of some part of a cash consideration is that it allows them to retain a hold over the sellers. For example, it can be seen as a way of making sure that the seller recognises legitimate claims under warranties and indemnities. Furthermore, deferral can allow the buyer to generate profits, including profits from the target business itself, to complete the financing of the acquisition. As a result, the initial need for borrowings is reduced.

Nonetheless, a seller faces a particular difficulty under a deferred consideration arrangement. Taxation liabilities on capital gains are calculated at the time of sale on the full consideration to be received in cash. Only on grounds of genuine hardship are exceptions made to this rule. Consequently, a buyer might have to make some concession to a seller in order to secure the benefits of deferred payment arrangements.

There are even stronger commercial reasons for a buyer to make payments which are related to post-acquisition performance. Contingent consideration is a way of reducing risk by ensuring that the amount paid for a business is directly related to its worth. It is also a useful motivator when the seller continues to be involved in the target business after acquisition. Nevertheless, as in the case of deferred consideration, the commercial advantages to the buyer may have to be paid for, because of the tax disadvantage imposed on the seller.

The Inland Revenue ascribes a value to the right to receive contingent cash payments and includes this in the initial sales proceeds. Although there will be a subsequent adjustment to reflect the actual payments that are made, the seller still has to pay tax in the first instance on a cash consideration which may never be received. With appropriate planning this problem can be avoided. Where deferred or contingent consideration takes the form of shares or debentures issued by the buyer, the key is take advantage of the Section 85 relief we discussed earlier and ensure that the seller's gains are only taxed on the ultimate sale of the consideration shares.

12.

ACCOUNTING CONSEQUENCES

12.1 THE IMPORTANCE OF ACCOUNTING

We have already introduced the various structures that can be used for an acquisition: a company buys shares or assets by issuing shares or debt or by paying in cash. In this chapter we explain how such transactions should be accounted for by the buying company, whether it has an existing business or is a vehicle for a management buy-out or buy-in team.

The way that acquisitions are structured has developed to take advantage of the accounting rules. In particular, certain roundabout transactions are entered into so that so-called "merger accounting" can be used in situations which were never intended by the rule-makers. Indeed, it may be thought that buying a business can be accounted for with such flexibility that, regardless of whether a purchase has been a success, it does at least look like a success in the accounts.

Those who might be intending to make a career out of such illusions should however be warned that the accounting and disclosure rules are under much review and are only likely to become tighter. Furthermore, although the buyer's reported profits may not reveal the economic reality of an overpriced or strategically ill-conceived acquisition, they cannot do so for ever or conceal the cash flow effects. A sound method of valuation remains of overriding importance in establishing whether the price of an acquisition is sensible.

12.2 COUNTING THE COST

The first issue we encounter is that of calculating the cost of an acquisition. Until we come to merger accounting later in the chapter, the answers follow common sense. The cost of an acquisition comprises the professional and other costs directly attributable to the acquisition and the fair value of the consideration paid to the seller.

There is little difficulty if the consideration is fixed, even though it may include deferred consideration which is not payable immediately. Where shares are issued instead of cash, there is usually a market price which can be used. In rare instances however where unquoted shares are part of the consideration, the values to be used may need to be in line with values which are acceptable to the Inland Revenue in determining the sales proceeds of the seller.

Contingent consideration presents additional challenges. In earn-out deals, where payments to sellers are related to post-acquisition earnings, judgement as well as patience is required in determining the fair value of the consideration. The fair value comprises two elements: a certain minimum consideration which is usually due immediately; and the additional consideration which crystallises under the earn-out agreement. Consequently, the cost of an acquisition has to be adjusted as the earn-out payments are calculated.

Judgement is called for to identify cases where earn-out payments effectively include some remuneration for management services provided by the sellers. Such amounts are really not part of the cost of acquiring the target business and should instead be deducted in calculating the post-acquisition profits of the target. This is a sensitive area because any buyer will want an acquisition to look a success and that means reporting high post-acquisition profits.

12.3 ASSET PURCHASES

Initially, we consider buying a business through a purchase of assets from a company, partnership or individual, rather than through a purchase of shares in a company. In this case the accounting is comparatively straightforward.

Once the consideration has been established, it must be allocated to the individual elements of the net assets acquired. This can involve revaluing certain items, such as fixed assets and stocks, and attributing values to other previously unvalued items such as patents and tooling. The balance that cannot be so allocated, the premium that has been paid, is described as purchased goodwill. If contingent consideration is involved, the value of this goodwill rises as each additional payment is calculated.

Purchased goodwill adversely affects distributable reserves. These reserves comprise the amounts of profit realised in the past which can be paid out to shareholders by way of dividend. Under UK Statement of Standard Accounting Practice No. 22, it is preferable to write off purchased goodwill immediately against distributable reserves. This one-off write-off will not be reflected in the profit for the year in which it occurs. Alternatively, purchased goodwill may be written off through the profit and loss account over a reasonable number of years, in which case it will be reflected in calculating the profits for those years. The number of years involved should reflect management's estimate of the "useful economic life" of the goodwill concerned.

Although purchased goodwill must be written off at some time for the purpose of preparing accounts, it is not allowed as a deduction in arriving at taxable profits. There is therefore a clear tax-saving motivation for a buyer to minimise the value attributable to goodwill and maximise the values attributable to tax deductible items.

Limits to the minimisation of goodwill are established by the accounting principle that fair and recoverable values should be attributed to the assets acquired. A buyer should consider obtaining professional valuations to support an allocation of the purchase consideration if it is felt that the allocation could be challenged by the tax authorities. The Inland Revenue will also not want to find their entitlement to tax being eroded by an unrealistically low goodwill value and it should be appreciated that an allocation of the purchase consideration which brings a tax benefit to the buyer will in general involve a tax cost to the seller.

12.4 SHARE PURCHASES

When a business is bought by the purchase of shares in a company carrying on that business, then the accounting becomes more complex. One complication is that a fundamental distinction has to be drawn between the buyer's own accounts, which show the buying company on its own, and the buyer's consolidated accounts, which show the buying and the target companies together. Moreover, there are two principal ways of accounting for a share purchase in both the buyer's own accounts and the consolidated accounts.

The alternatives, which are known as "acquisition accounting" and "merger accounting", should not be thought of as alternative ways of accounting for the same transaction but as different ways of accounting for different types of transaction. Broadly, merger accounting is only allowed by law and UK accounting standards when all or almost all of the share capital of the target is acquired and the consideration consists entirely or almost entirely of shares in the buyer. In these circumstances, two sets of shareholders are effectively pooling their interests and the resources of the combining businesses are not being depleted to any significant extent. Acquisition accounting may be applied in these circumstances and must be applied in all other circumstances. We describe acquisition accounting first.

12.5 ACQUISITION ACCOUNTING

With a purchase of business assets, the initial task was to establish the fair value of the consideration given. When acquisition accounting for the purchase of a company we have to do the same thing and find the fair value of the consideration. This value appears in the buying company's balance sheet as the cost of a fixed asset investment, namely the target company's shares.

There are no laid down rules as to how the value of the fixed asset investment should later be adjusted to reflect the subsequent profits and losses of the company that has been bought or the write-off of any goodwill where there is an excess of the purchase consideration over the value of the target's identifiable net assets. However, no matter what subsequent adjustments are made to revalue an investment in a subsidiary, in general, an acquisition can only increase the distributable reserves of the buying company when the subsidiary pays dividends out of profits earned after the acquisition. Distributable reserves are the amounts that a company can legally pay out to shareholders by way of dividend.

Any dividends paid by a subsidiary are deemed to be paid firstly out of any post-acquisition retained profits and then out of pre-acquisition profits. Dividends paid out of pre-acquisition profits will usually be deducted from the cost of the fixed asset investment and will not be added to the buying company's distributable reserves. An exception can arise when the directors of the buying company form the considered view that no reduction is required because, even after the payment of the dividend, the value of the investment in the subsidiary has not fallen below the cost at which it is stated in their accounts.

Although an acquisition will not in itself increase the distributable reserves of the buying company, it is also unlikely to reduce these reserves. Such a reduction only occurs if that part of the consideration which represents goodwill, and not the underlying net assets of the target, is actually written off in the buying company's own accounts. Such a treatment would be voluntary.

We turn now from the buyer's own accounts to the consolidated accounts under acquisition accounting. The consolidated balance sheet cannot show the fixed asset investment at all. Instead, the fair value of the consideration given to acquire the target company, which is the value of the fixed asset investment, will be allocated to reflect the individual assets and liabilities of the target. Thus the investment disappears but the fair values of the subsidiary's fixed assets, stocks, debtors, cash and creditors are added to the holding company's in determining the balances to be shown against these captions in the consolidated balance sheet.

12.6 THE IMPLICATIONS OF "ACQUISITION"

In acquisition accounting, as in the case of buying business assets, goodwill is the name given to that portion of the total consideration which cannot be allocated to tangible net assets, such as fixed assets, stocks, debtors less creditors, cash and even "brands". In this context, although it is called "goodwill arising on consolidation" rather than "purchased goodwill", the accounting treatment is broadly the same. Goodwill arising on consolidation must be written off immediately against reserves or over a number of years against profits.

The consolidation process and the consolidation treatment of goodwill have no effect on the buying company's distributable reserves under acquisition accounting. Distributable reserves are affected only by the accounting treatment adopted in the buying company's own accounts and, in particular, by whether the goodwill element of the consideration is voluntarily written off against these reserves.

A buyer with a weak consolidated balance sheet, whether because of a small net asset value or high gearing, is unlikely to welcome a large goodwill write-off in the consolidated accounts. Such write-offs further reduce shareholders' funds and increase gearing and they are a reason for the popularity of ascribing value to a target's brands. By valuing brands, a buyer reduces the amount of goodwill arising on consolidation.

On the other hand, for a buyer with a strong balance sheet, there is a temptation to underestimate the fair value of the underlying net assets of the target, for example by making excessive provisions for reorganisation costs. This has the effect of increasing the goodwill which can be written off on acquisition without being reflected in reported earnings or distributable profits. At the same time future earnings are strengthened if reorganisation and other costs are recognised unnecessarily or prematurely.

The buyer with a strong balance sheet may also become recklessly unconcerned about paying too much for an acquisition. After all, any extra outlay can be written off immediately against reserves with no apparent effect on future earnings. It is easy to overlook the additional and unnecessary financing costs that will be involved and which will affect earnings.

Before moving on to merger accounting, we summarise the salient points from our description of acquisition accounting.

1. The distributable reserves of the buying company do not have to be reduced by the write-off of goodwill as they do when business assets are bought.
2. The only increase in distributable reserves in the buying company occurs when dividends are paid up from the target company out of profits earned after acquisition. The pre-acquisition profits of the target are said to become "frozen" and do not even appear in the consolidated balance sheet.
3. Goodwill acquired through the purchase of a company cannot forever remain in the consolidated balance sheet.

12.7 MERGER ACCOUNTING

Under UK Statement of Standard Accounting Practice No. 23, merger accounting is only permitted under certain circumstances. These are where an offer is made by a company holding less than 20 per cent of the target's equity to the rest of the target's shareholders. As a result of this offer, the company must hold 90 per cent or more of the target's equity. Furthermore, at least 90 per cent of the total consideration given to acquire that total holding must be in the form of shares.

It is for these reasons that the roundabout transactions discussed in Chapter 9 may be used. Initial purchases of shares in a target may be made through a friendly intermediary or sold on to such an intermediary to ensure that when the buyer subsequently makes an offer for the target's shares, it holds less than 20 per cent. The vendor placing route may be taken to ensure that at least 90 per cent of the consideration given is in the form of shares, even though the sellers want and ultimately receive cash.

In considering merger accounting, we will for simplicity be referring throughout to a pure exchange of shares where the buying company acquires all the shares of the target company and in exchange issues new shares in itself. We will highlight the differences from acquisition accounting by considering first the buying company's own accounts.

The fair value of the consideration given by the buying company does not need to be established under merger accounting as it does under acquisition accounting. In the buying company's balance sheet it is the nominal value of the shares issued by the buying company which appears and not the often much larger fair market value of those shares.

This small nominal value is treated as the cost of the buying company's fixed asset investment in the acquired company.

Turning to the consolidated balance sheet, this does not show the small fixed asset investment at all. The investment disappears, to be replaced on the net assets side of the consolidated balance sheet not by the fair values but by the book values of the acquired company's fixed assets, stock, debtors and cash less creditors. On the other side of the consolidated balance sheet, the shareholders' funds side, all the reserves of the acquired company are shown, subject to an adjustment to reflect the difference between the share capital of the target company and the nominal value of the buyer's share issue.

12.8 FEATURES OF "MERGERS"

The exciting news for those who were depressed by the effects of acquisition accounting is that there is no need for large goodwill write-offs. This is clearly popular when targets are bought which have little asset-backing. When an advertising agency is acquired, the goodwill involved can be very large. In addition, the consolidated balance sheet shows the reserves of the acquired company. Any dividends paid to the buying company out of pre-acquisition profits can be added to the buying company's distributable reserves and are not deducted from the cost of the fixed asset investment as was the case under acquisition accounting.

Furthermore, as fair current values have not been attributed to the target company's fixed assets, depreciation charges will continue to be based on the historic cost of those assets. Accordingly, the consolidated profit and loss account is not hit by the significantly increased depreciation charge which customarily arises under acquisition accounting. In addition, the balance sheet will not contain a mixture of historic costs and subsequent fair values.

To summarise, merger accounting is very popular for two reasons.

1. The distributable reserves of both the buyer and the target are left largely intact.
2. Future earnings are not depressed through increased depreciation charges and the amortisation of goodwill.

Merger accounting is further distinguished from acquisition accounting because the results of the buyer prior to the merger are adjusted as if the merger had always been in force. Under acquisition accounting, the results of the buying company and the target business are only combined for the period after the acquisition.

12.9 MERGER RELIEF

So far, we have argued that acquisition accounting has its attractions to those who have a robust balance sheet and see the opportunity to boost post-acquisition performance by maximising the goodwill write-off on acquisition. As a result, the earnings of buyers who use acquisition accounting can show exceptional growth, especially in view of the fact that only the target's post-acquisition results are included in the buyer's consolidated earnings record. The desire to use merger accounting rather than acquisition accounting is particularly strong when a service sector business is bought, because when the target has little asset-backing the large goodwill write-off may devastate the buyer's consolidated balance sheet. There is however a final quirk of company law which can help to make acquisition accounting more attractive even when large goodwill write-offs are in prospect.

To understand the issue, we must return to our discussion of merger accounting, where we noted that a buying company does not have to record in its balance sheet the fair value of the shares it issues, merely their nominal value. The legal provisions to allow this were actually introduced to permit merger accounting but they apply more widely, indeed whenever a buyer makes a share issue which results in the buyer owning at least 90 per cent of a target. In other circumstances where this "merger relief" does not apply, the fair value of the shares must be recorded with any excess over the nominal value being shown as a share premium account, the use of which is highly restricted.

It has become normal to take advantage of the "merger relief" provisions and so avoid setting up a share premium account even when merger accounting is not allowed and acquisition accounting is being followed. Instead of creating a share premium account, companies set up a "merger relief reserve" and use it to write off items, including acquisition costs and goodwill. In the absence of merger relief, such items could not be written off against a share premium account and would therefore have adversely affected other reserves. Acquisition accounting with merger relief has consequently become a very popular option although its continued availability cannot be assured.

13.

LEGAL PROTECTION

13.1 LEGAL MEANS AND ENDS

In this chapter, we look at six forms of legal protection for limiting the risks facing the buyer of a business.

1. Conditional terms
2. The tie-in of key employees
3. Restrictive covenants
4. The hive-down
5. Warranties and indemnities
6. Retention arrangements

These devices must be kept in context. They are not the crutches upon which a disorganised management should rely to resolve all the key issues of the acquisition process. Moreover, it should be appreciated from the outset that when buying a quoted company, the scope for using any of the means of legal protection is severely limited and in practice only certain conditional terms may be available.

The means we discuss form part of a planned programme to address issues during the strategy and search phases, during the buying process itself and in the aftermath of an acquisition. The full picture is brought together in the Issues Management Guide in Appendix I. The buying management team must take an intelligent and active interest in the matters discussed in this chapter and must not regard them either as ends in themselves or as the esoteric nit-picking means which professional advisers employ to justify their fees.

13.2 CONDITIONAL TERMS

A useful starting point in limiting risk is to make the terms of an agreement conditional upon future events.

On the one hand, the amount of the purchase consideration can be made conditional upon the post-acquisition performance of the acquired business. An earn-out agreement along these lines might involve a basic payment for net assets at the date of acquisition with further payments being calculated by reference to the profits of, for example, the first three subsequent years. Although such an arrangement can cause its own difficulties, it is a means of limiting risk.

A drawback of contingent payment arrangements is that, even if subsequent results are thoroughly audited, a seller is going to be unenthusiastic if denied a significant influence on the management and financial reporting of the business during the period when the contingent payments are determined. A seller will not want to suffer because the buyer manages the acquisition badly or siphons off profits into another business.

The buyer on the other hand may not be prepared to tolerate the interference of the seller unless the seller is somebody whose services and commitment are needed to make a success of the acquisition. In the buyer's eyes, a seller may also become obstructive in the face of any imaginative but risky or long-term initiatives as these could threaten profitability during the period when contingent payments are determined by profits. Such initiatives may however be necessary if the original purpose of the acquisition is to be fulfilled.

Alternatively, not just the consideration, but the acquisition deal itself can be made conditional. The entire offer made to the sellers of a business, can be made conditional upon specific "disasters" not occurring. An example of a specific "disaster", which the buyer of a public target is obliged to cover in this way, is a referral to the Monopolies and Mergers Commission. Furthermore, an agreement to acquire a private company can be reached but completion can be made dependent upon the fulfilment of certain conditions. This approach addresses the two contrasting risks that: until there is some agreement, a seller can always walk away; and unless completion is made conditional, a buyer could find that a deal has gone through on a basis which is unacceptable. The benefits need to be weighed against the difficulties that can arise in deciding how to manage the target in the period between the agreement and completion.

13.3 THE TIE-IN OF KEY EMPLOYEES

It is not only an individual seller whose continued involvement in the target business may be important to a buyer's plans. The buyer should also identify key employees and consider using a variety of means to eliminate risks concerning their continued employment and motivation. Prior to an acquisition, the risk may be that they will frustrate the potential buyer's plans by organising a management buy-out alternative to the purchase. If such efforts have been undertaken seriously then the advisability of any subsequent acquisition should be questioned, although because the popularity of buy-outs has grown so much this should not be seen as an unusual or prohibitive occurence.

After an acquisition, key individuals can be insured against death or illness and, to an extent, tied in to working for the business by service contracts or consultancy arrangements. However, these contracts are for personal services and cannot be specifically enforced: a court will not order an employee to work for an employer in accordance with a contract of employment. Nevertheless, a service contract may have the benefit of imposing moral pressure on an employee not to break its terms. It may also form the basis of a claim for damages for breach of contract if an employee leaves, even though employers very rarely seek to claim such damages because they are usually limited to the cost of hiring a replacement.

In order to ensure that key employees are not only at work but also working effectively there must be a strong element of performance-related reward whether in the form of bonus, share option or share incentive schemes. Furthermore, where the seller is also a key manager, an earn-out is not the only solution. The immediate payment of the purchase consideration by means of shares in the enlarged business could contribute greatly towards continued motivation. Provided that the manager cannot sell the consideration shares too quickly, there is an incentive to build up profits and so boost the value of the shares.

Alternatively, an owner-manager can be left as a minority shareholder in the target company. The seller would remain committed to the continuing success of the company since further gains could be realised in the future if the buyer sought to acquire the remainder of the shares. Nonetheless, in the meantime, the buyer's freedom of action may be limited by the seller's rights as a minority shareholder.

13.4 RESTRICTIVE COVENANTS

The buyer of a business faces a major risk that the seller of the target business or a key employee will set up in competition. In effect, the seller or an employee could make use of goodwill which has supposedly already been sold to the buyer. To eliminate such an uncertainty, the buyer should make sure that a private acquisition agreement contains a covenant not to compete and that key employees also enter into such covenants.

A covenant not to compete is itself open to two sorts of risk and therefore requires careful drafting. First, if it is unreasonable either in its scope or duration, it will be invalid at common law as a restraint of trade. Second, a covenant not to compete may fall foul of legislation to limit restrictive practices.

The restrictive trade practices legislation has required registration of agreements where two or more parties carrying on a business in the UK accept restrictions on their business activities. Once registered, an agreement is referred to The Restrictive Practices Court which can declare it void if it is considered contrary to the public interest. This should not present a major risk where an acquisition agreement only involves an undertaking by one party, the seller, not to compete. It has also been possible to seek a declaration that an agreement is of "minor significance" and does not need to be referred to the Court.

13.5 THE HIVE-DOWN

The hive-down involves a seller transferring a trading activity to a new subsidiary company for the purpose of selling it. This can be attractive when a seller wishes to sell shares in a company for tax reasons but buyers are wary of the skeletons that they could inherit if the seller's existing company is bought. For these reasons, the hive-down used to be common in receiverships. However, since the 1986 Budget the additional tax benefits of such hive-downs have been greatly reduced.

Nevertheless, where a buyer is wary of skeletons, both parties can still benefit from a hive-down. A hive-down is also attractive from a commercial point of view to a seller who is carrying on several separately saleable businesses through a single company. If each business is hived down into a separate company, the seller might be able to secure the potential tax benefits of a share sale on the disposal of each business.

The most straightforward way to carry out a hive-down is simply to transfer the trading activity and the related assets to be sold to a 100 per cent subsidiary company which is subsequently sold. If the transfer is made to a newly incorporated company, then the buyer need not worry about skeletons from the past. However, care is needed to make sure that the hive-down is carried out without involving a tax cost.

13.6 WARRANTIES AND INDEMNITIES

During the buying process, the buyer relies on the representations of the target's management in assessing the riskiness and value of the target. For example, representations are often made about the collectibility of debtors and compliance with tax legislation. The buyer needs to be properly protected if these representations, which have been borne in mind when settling the price, turn out to have been wrong.

The purchaser is however frequently unable to bring any action for misrepresentation. This is the case where the seller inserts a clause into the contract for the sale of a business stating that the buyer is only relying on those representations which are the subject of warranties.

A warranty arises when the vendor makes a representation in the contract for sale about the business being sold. Rescission of the contract may be possible in the case of a breach of warranty which is fundamental to the contract, for example, if there was a compulsory purchase order on the target's place of business or a key patent was invalid. Once a contract has been completed, rescission is very difficult because it involves restoring the status quo. Nevertheless, in cases where there is a gap between the exchange of contracts and the completion, perhaps for the satisfaction of certain conditions, then rescission of the contract is a very real remedy. Such a remedy should be specifically provided for so that a purchaser can avoid having to complete if something material happens.

The other remedy for breach of warranty is damages. The sum involved in a claim for breach of contract is the difference between the price paid and the value which is judged to have been received by the purchaser. With claims of negligence, the damages are intended to put purchasers in the same position as if they had not entered into any purchase contract. Payment of the actual loss incurred by the purchaser can be obtained where an indemnity is invoked.

A deed of indemnity sets out those circumstances in which the seller will make good a financial loss of the buyer. Indemnities are invariably sought for certain taxation liabilities and they may also be used, for example, to cover the costs of product recalls and returns arising from pre-acquisition sales.

A common difficulty which a buyer needs to face concerns who should give warranties and indemnities. A target company often has outside shareholders who do not participate in the active management of the business and who are therefore not in a position to verify the representations given to the buyer. In general, it is perfectly reasonable for the buyer to insist that any selling shareholders give warranties and indemnities since it is they who are receiving the purchase consideration which is being underpinned by those warranties and indemnities. They are also more likely to have the financial resources to meet any claims.

Management buy-out teams can however experience particular resistance if the sellers argue that the management should know everything there is to know about the target. This is unlikely to be true in areas such as capital structure, property and pensions if such matters have been handled by a head office or holding company. Nevertheless, on operational matters management should be prepared to be more flexible in seeking warranties and indemnities.

Although it is on warranties and indemnities that the purchaser will rely in seeking redress in a private acquisition, they do not obviate the need for proper investigation into the target business. Warranties and indemnities may be particularly hard to enforce if the seller is a company which goes into liquidation or an individual who retires abroad. In addition, there is no compensation for the considerable management time and expense that is likely to be involved in pursuing such remedies in law, although a successful plaintiff could be awarded costs and a contract can provide, in the warranty and indemnity provisions, that costs incurred in enforcing any claims will be covered.

One possible solution to concerns about enforcing warranties and indemnities is to seek insurance. It is worth considering if the buyer is paying in full for the acquisition upfront or if the sellers are not people of financial substance.

13.7 THE SCOPE OF WARRANTIES AND INDEMNITIES

The risks to be addressed by contractual provision arise in all the areas that we will identify in due course as areas for investigation. For instance, a contract for the purchase of either business assets or shares usually calls for warranties covering the accuracy of reported earnings, the recoverability of asset values, the condition of fixed assets, the adequacy of the vendor's title to the property being sold and the completeness of schedules detailing obligations to employees.

In the case of a purchase of shares, the matters covered by warranties also include compliance with company law, contractual obligations, current litigation and, perhaps most importantly, taxation. Tax warranties address risks of non-compliance with legislation, inadequate provision for liabilities in the target's accounts, and the special dangers which can arise where the target is leaving a group. These warranties are also normally supplemented by a deed of indemnity covering all taxation liabilities not provided for at the date of the agreement which are attributable to pre-acquisition activities.

The extensive provisions relevant to a share purchase can result in a contract and deed of indemnity covering a hundred pages or more. In addition, information referred to in the warranties and exceptions to the warranties will be set out in a disclosure letter from the seller. The buyer should ensure that drafts of these complex and important documents are available and updated on a prompt and comprehensive basis throughout the buying process.

In the area of warranties and indemnities, the traffic is not entirely one way. The purchaser will probably have to give as well as take, especially when the purchaser issues shares to effect the acquisition. The seller will also usually look for a tax indemnity covering any prejudicial actions by the purchaser which could adversely affect the seller's tax position.

Furthermore, when giving warranties and indemnities, it is common for sellers to try to restrict their financial exposure to the price received by them, even though this may be less than a purchaser's subsequent loss. If there is a group of sellers, they can divide up the potential liability amongst themselves by a separate agreement. Sellers also like to make the wordings of warranties and indemnities as specific as possible and to limit the time period covered, for example, to three and six years respectively. These are nonetheless entirely matters for negotiation.

Finally, as mentioned earlier, the seller usually seeks an admission that all representations on which the buyer has relied are the subject of warranties. A clause to this effect may protect the seller from liability for misrepresentation but it is not certain that it will be effective.

It helps the seller's case if negotiations and correspondence make it clear that the purchaser is expected to specify in the contract those representations upon which reliance is being placed. In such circumstances, a heavier responsibility is placed on the buyer's professional advisers to identify all the areas where contractual provision is necessary. However, in general, the framing of warranties and indemnities can serve a useful purpose in flushing out issues which, for whatever reason, have not been properly covered by investigation. For convenient reference, we have outlined in Appendix III the contractual warranties and indemnities that might be sought in a private company purchase.

13.8 RETENTION ARRANGEMENTS

Retentions are distinct from deferred consideration arrangements, under which the seller is effectively helping to finance an acquisition, and earn-out deals, where the consideration is contingent upon the post-acquisition performance of the target. Retention arrangements are merely intended to make warranties and indemnities effective.

If a buyer is placing heavy reliance on the warranties and indemnities given by the seller, it is common to hold back some part of the purchase consideration to cover potential claims. As with warranty and indemnity insurance, this is particularly wise if a seller is about to emigrate or is thought to have limited resources. A retention is also a common safeguard if the target company is subject to some major litigation, bad debt risk or tax negotiation.

The release of a retention may occur on a specified date after completion or it may be dependent on the occurrence of some event set out in the sale agreement. Retentions are difficult to put in place when all of the consideration is to be in the form of shares since cash is the only easily retained asset. The cash involved is commonly held in a joint bank account in the names of the buyer's and seller's solicitors who can only deal with the money in accordance with the sale agreement or the instructions of both their clients. Interest which accrues on the retention account is generally paid over to the seller.

14.

INVESTIGATION

14.1 THE PURPOSE OF INVESTIGATION

The purpose of investigation activity is to gather information for use in the other activities of the buying process. The scope for performing investigation work is usually limited when the target is a public company and this is especially so if the acquisition attempt is unwelcome. It is an essential feature of public securities markets that all buyers and sellers of shares should have access to the same information and publicly quoted companies are subject to regulations covering the disclosure of information.

The principle of common information can however come into conflict with the requirement that directors should act in the interests of their shareholders. The directors of a quoted company may believe that if they are not to stifle a bid which may be beneficial to their shareholders then they must disclose, on a confidential basis, certain non-public information to a potential buyer. Close consultation with financial advisers is called for before taking action in this sensitive area.

The different types of investigation activity concern us in the rest of this chapter while Appendix II and the three succeeding chapters are devoted to the matters to be investigated.

14.2 TYPES OF INVESTIGATION

Investigation work is usually carried out by a firm of independent professional accountants, such as the buying company's auditors, and it can take a variety of forms. Most aspects of acquisition work involve the auditor in abandoning the time-honoured role as "more of a watchdog than a bloodhound", to become more of a bloodhound.

We identify three different types of exercise, all of which the investigating accountants could perform in relation to a single acquisition and all of which can result in the production of a report.

1. Pre-purchase review
2. Purchase investigation
3. Acquisition audit

The idea behind identifying the three separate exercises which are the subject of this chapter is not to maximise the cost to the potential purchaser: far from it. The aim is to prevent the purchaser from wasting money and the money-saving principle involved is simple. It can be extremely wasteful for the investigating accountants to perform a single large expensive exercise. Such an exercise might identify a myriad of minor points to be reflected in the final consideration and the warranties and indemnities. It may also identify more significant matters which would require major revisions to the form and terms of the purchase agreement. Finally, it could identify a few major problems which make an acquisition inconceivable.

It is far more sensible to perform a series of shorter and less expensive exercises to suit the purposes of management as they pursue an acquisition target. To ensure therefore that time and money are not wasted on unnecessary work it is advisable for the potential buyer to define and confirm in writing terms of reference for all the work to be performed by the investigating accountants. To assist in this process, Appendix II sets out the areas which may be investigated by a buyer prior to purchase and it can be used to determine the scope of both the pre-purchase review and the purchase investigation.

Although the money-saving principle which we have referred to will always be relevant, it must be admitted that a distinct phasing of the investigating accountants' work is sometimes not practical on smaller acquisitions.

14.3 THE PRE-PURCHASE REVIEW

The pre-purchase review is a quick exercise to collect financial and business information about the target. The information is not subjected to detailed verification but is intended to provide the potential buyer with a better understanding of the target, its industry and the reasons why it is for sale.

As a result of the pre-purchase review, it might be concluded that the target really does not fit the acquisition profile or that the target does not represent a good buy, for example, if it is in a market with poor long-term prospects or if it is operationally so efficient that there would be little scope for achieving higher profits than those already reflected in the asking price. The pre-purchase review should also reveal any fundamental problems or "skeletons in the cupboard" which would persuade the potential buyer to withdraw.

The specific and limited role of the pre-purchase review should always be borne in mind. Frequently, such a review is not successful in obtaining the information necessary for a proper evaluation of the candidate and a sound decision about whether to continue. Poor results may stem from bad communication, lack of careful planning or a failure by the potential purchasers and their investigating accountants to fix responsibilities and co-ordinate their efforts. However, and perhaps most importantly, the review may focus on the quantity rather than the quality of the information obtained so that significant facts either get lost in a sea of paper or never get collected.

Many accounting firms use detailed checklists of questions which they use in their pre-purchase reviews. Checklists should be tailored to fit the risks specific to each acquisition target. It is easy to mistake a list of "not applicable" or superficial responses for useful work. Appendix II lists the matters which should be considered for investigation in the UK and, by its length, it illustrates the dangers of checklists. The buyer should limit the scope of the work to be performed to exclude areas of low risk and those areas where the buyer already has considerable knowledge. Our checklist is also drafted so that it does not merely require the investigating accountant to collect a mass of documents. The salient points must be extracted and their implications presented to the potential buyer.

A pitfall of the pre-purchase review is that it can be seen as a substitute for proper strategic thinking and search activity. It may be left to the investigating accountants to point out the basic commercial inadvisability of a proposed acquisition. This is especially dangerous if the investigating accountants are unaware of the burden being placed on them. It also represents a waste of resources and brings with it the risk that management will make themselves look foolish in front of a wide audience of professional advisers and target company personnel.

14.4 THE PURCHASE INVESTIGATION

The purchase investigation should only be undertaken if, following the pre-purchase review, the potential buyer is still interested in acquiring the target. The principal aim of the purchase investigation is to identify significant matters which will either be reflected in the valuation of the target or in the warranties and indemnities sought by the purchaser.

It is preferable if the seller and target work closely with the investigating accountants during the purchase investigation. As well as containing the costs of the exercise, such co-operation gives the buyer a chance to assess the credibility and competence of the seller and target, while ensuring that misunderstandings do not drift into the purchase investigation report and so cloud subsequent negotiations. Whether the seller or target should see the investigation report itself is a different matter. It is however useful if the factual content of a report can be reviewed by the "other side" without the judgements being disclosed. The disclosure of judgements does not just raise emotions, it also weakens the buyer's bargaining stance by highlighting attractive aspects of the target and giving advance warning of areas in which the buyer will seek to talk the price down.

The pre-purchase review provides a high level assessment of the key risks and opportunities inherent in the target's business, its current position and its past performance. The purchase investigation involves collecting more detailed information on the strengths and weaknesses of the business and its management and embraces a more thorough review of the target's financial accounting records. Once more, it is for the buyer to determine the areas of particular concern and to define the scope of the work to be performed.

The purchase investigation is still quite distinct from an audit. Although verification work is performed, the investigating accountants are not in a position to express an opinion on the truth and fairness of all the information they gather and present in their report. Nevertheless, the special purpose report which results from the purchase investigation is more wide-ranging than a set of audited financial statements. It contains, at a minimum, a commentary covering accounting policies and the subjective and uncertain issues relating to individual account captions.

One aspect of a purchase investigation which is frequently required but which cannot result in a "true and fair" opinion from the accountants is a review of the target's financial projections. These may range from a fairly accurate forecast of the outturn of the present accounting period to a set of profit and loss, balance sheet and cashflow projections covering the next five years. Such projections are essential reading for anyone who is concerned with the valuation of the target and the ability of the buyers to justify and finance the acquisition.

The investigating accountants need to confirm the appropriateness of the accounting policies used and the clerical accuracy of the projections. More importantly however they should point out the key commercial assumptions which underpin the projections and the sensitivity of projected performance to changes in these assumptions. In this way the accountants will enable the buyers and potential investors to probe the quality of the target's earnings and assess the risk of the target business.

14.5 THE ACQUISITION AUDIT

A final service offered by a firm of independent professional accountants is the acquisition audit. This option is not available when acquiring a quoted company. In recognition of this, the buyer may even want to discount the value of the net assets shown in the balance sheet of a quoted company to anticipate adjustments which might have resulted from an audit by the buyer's investigating accountants. In other situations, when buying a private company or part of a public group, it is important to recognise when an acquisition audit may or may not be desirable.

A buyer might not require an acquisition audit where the investigating accountants have already performed both a pre-purchase review and a purchase investigation and the target company's auditors are performing a statutory audit at or near the agreement date. The buyer's decision could stem from a desire to contain professional fees and to avoid generating ill-feeling within the target's management.

However, when the purchase consideration is to reflect adjustments to asset values on a pound for pound basis, the buyer is often prepared to accept the costs involved and have an audit performed. The investigating accountants may also be the buyer's current auditors and the target's future auditors. It is therefore important that they are instructed to perform sufficient work on the target's balance sheet at the acquisition date to enable them to give a "clean opinion" in their audit report on the subsequent profit and loss account. Indeed, it is often commercially unacceptable to have anything but a clean opinion on the target's accounts and the buyer's consolidated accounts.

If an acquisition audit is requested, the investigating accountants need to express an opinion as to whether a set of accounts prepared at the acquisition date gives a true and fair view of the target's financial position. They will be fully responsible for that opinion, irrespective of the statutory auditors' involvement.

If a statutory audit is in progress at the time of a proposed acquisition, the investigating accountants can, for practical reasons, be instructed to perform sufficient work to confirm that the target's auditors have complied with the auditing profession's approved standards. Such work typically includes attendance at stockcounts and a thorough review of the statutory auditors' working papers. The review should pay particular attention to areas of risk identified in the pre-purchase review and purchase investigation reports. Any additional audit procedures that the investigating accountants consider necessary, in areas of special concern to a buyer, are normally discharged by the investigating accountants themselves with the results being communicated directly to the buyer.

Less straightforward are those instances in which the date of the purchase does not coincide with a statutory audit or where the target is not subject to audit, for example if it is a partnership or a division or branch of a company. In these circumstances it is likely that the purchaser will wish to have an audit performed. The target's professional advisers and, where applicable, the target's auditors may be of considerable assistance. Nonetheless, the investigating accountants are essentially on their own in an area where proper planning is essential.

14.6 PLANNING FOR THE ACQUISITION AUDIT

The scope of the audit must be carefully determined. Are the accountants to report merely on the balance sheet at the acquisition date or are they also expressing an opinion on profit and loss accounts and statements of source and application of funds? If they are reporting on the target's performance over a period of months or years, then they will need to audit or be satisfied with the audit of the balance sheet at the beginning of the period and this may not now be practical. For example, stock records might not exist to corroborate the stock balances shown in the opening balance sheet.

The form and content of the accounts need to be decided with the target's management who are responsible for their preparation. The accounts need not comply with company legislation since they will not constitute statutory annual accounts and, besides, some statutory disclosure requirements would not be relevant to the purchaser.

There is generally agreement that the accounts should contain all and only the information relevant to the buyer. Indeed, the investigating accountants will probably say that their own report has only been provided for the purposes of the proposed acquisition and should not be used for other purposes without their written consent. Nonetheless, the buyer should make sure that the investigating accountants understand clearly what is considered relevant and useful for the purposes of making the acquisition.

A final and occasionally entertaining task is to decide by what authority the investigating accountants contact third parties in seeking audit evidence. Furthermore, how are their activities to be presented to the target's employees so as not to arouse unnecessary hostility or suspicion? The accountants may have to be prepared to accommodate the target's wishes as to how they are described so as not to cause alarm.

It is important to prepare in advance a timetable for reporting the results of the audit. This timetable should reconcile possible commercial needs for a speedy conclusion of the purchase with the investigating accountants' need to complete procedures involving the receipt of confirmations from third parties and the review of post balance sheet events. Certainly, if the audit is worth doing then it is worth doing properly. All the same, those concerned should remember that the ultimate relevance of the audit work depends upon its likely impact on the consideration and the purchase contract.

During the following three chapters we consider the major areas of risk which should concern the investigators throughout their work.

15.

UNDERSTANDING THE TARGET BUSINESS

15.1 INTERPRETING THE PAST AND THE PRESENT

Throughout their work on a potential acquisition, the investigating accountants are seeking to understand the historical results of the target, its likely future earnings and its present financial position. These are essential elements of any valuation and an understanding of the target's business and its previous management are crucial to any type of acquisition.

The accountants' work should also not be dismissed as irrelevant by a management buy-out team. Management may not appreciate how much their accounts have been distorted by the previous owners of the business and they may have come to accept things as normal practice which will look very different to outside investors when they are evaluating a deal and monitoring subsequent performance.

To succeed, the investigating accountants must focus their attention instead of recounting the past indiscriminately. In the context of a particular proposed purchase, the buyer and the investigator should identify specific areas of risk. We dwell on six possible areas of risk and these will demand that a buyer has a sound grasp of some basic accounting concepts.

1. Financial reporting objectives
2. Accounting policies
3. Window-dressing
4. Liquidity trends
5. Margin fluctuations
6. Related party transactions

15.2 THE REPORTING OF PAST RESULTS

It should be remembered that in the past the target business may have had specific financial reporting objectives. For instance, small unquoted companies sometimes adopt a very prudent approach in their accounts so as to minimise tax liabilities. Foreign-owned subsidiaries may smooth earnings between years so as to avoid embarrassing questions from the overseas parent. The results of small units within large groups may only have needed to be accurate within the materiality limits relevant to the group as a whole and their reported results should be viewed with great caution.

Consequently, the investigating accountants' work should be aimed, in a way that the normal work of auditors is not, at giving their client an impression of the quality of the target's net assets and reported earnings. This impression will affect the purchaser's view of reported performance and future prospects and thereby influence the valuation of the business.

An indispensable part of any work to assess the effect of financial reporting objectives would be a review of the target's approach to the determination of provisions. These include reserves both against assets such as stock, contract work-in-progress, debtors and investments and against uncertain liabilities such as deferred taxation, warranty claims and litigation. The adequacy or excessiveness of these provisions needs to be viewed in the light of the target's past experience, the risks inherent in the business and the reliance that can be placed upon management's estimates.

The target's accounting policies should also be compared with relevant industry practice and the potential buyer's own policies. Sensitive accounting issues to consider include exceptional and extraordinary items, goodwill, leasing, stock and long-term contract work-in-progress valuations, fixed asset revaluations, fixed asset depreciation rates, deferred tax, foreign currency translation and pension costs.

Until the advent of Statement of Standard Accounting Practice No.24, companies have had particular scope for "managing" their profits year by year by deciding when to make contributions to their pension schemes. This has been the case even where the real cost of providing pensions to employees has been being incurred quite regularly, year in and year out. It is therefore wise to isolate the pension costs appearing in the profit and loss account and to replace them with an appropriate ongoing charge.

By working out the effect of applying different accounting policies in all the areas we have listed, the investigating accountants can make a significant contribution to understanding the quality of the target's earnings and assets and the underlying trends in performance. In addition, any cost or benefit, in future profit terms, of bringing the target's accounting policies into line with those of the buyer needs to be made clear at the outset.

15.3 WINDOW-DRESSING

The consideration of reporting objectives and accounting policies leads us into a further area of concern. The investigating accountants should perform a wide-ranging and imaginative review to detect "window-dressing", either intentional or unintentional. The accountants may, for instance, tabulate the levels of key balances over recent years, including those for provisions and deferred expenditure, in order to identify any apparent distortion of earnings trends.

The main area of window-dressing is "off balance sheet finance". A major aim of this is to improve gearing, that is the ratio of debt to shareholders' funds, by removing from the balance sheet certain borrowings and the assets they are being used to finance. The leasing of fixed assets was the most common form of off balance sheet finance until the introduction of UK Statement of Standard Accounting Practice No.21. Regulatory attention is now being turned towards other abuses such as the hiving down of debt-financed properties into special subsidiaries which, for technical reasons, are not included in the parent company's consolidated balance sheet. The factoring of debts and the purchase of stocks on consignment can also distort the apparent liquidity and indebtedness of a company.

A further window-dressing possibility to consider is that profitability prior to the intended sale of a business could have been artificially improved. Costs can be saved by delaying advertising campaigns, research projects, product development plans or plant maintenance programmes. Tough decisions can be avoided or delayed. Sales can be boosted by deliberate efforts to clear out old stock lines or by threats of imminent price increases.

Attention should also be paid to cut-off dates for recording transactions in particular periods. For example, despatches or cash receipts occurring early in a period may have been recorded in the previous period. Another easily effected form of window-dressing involves inflating cash balances in a subsidiary which is being sold by moving funds around a group. In general, all unusual transactions prior to the sale or around the end of an accounting period should be scrutinised.

15.4 HISTORIC OPERATING ISSUES

The investigating accountants should be mindful of the liquidity trends highlighted by previous statements of source and application of funds. These statements should be adjusted to remove any window-dressing transactions that have been identified, any unusual points of presentation and any effects of off balance sheet finance.

An underlying deterioration in the liquidity position, when taken with current lease commitments, loan repayment terms and seasonal strains on liquidity, may indicate that a target will be unable to survive without financial support from a takeover. In such a forced sale, the potential buyer may be able to negotiate a much better deal.

Changes in margins and turnover levels in the periods and years prior to an acquisition should be matters of concern to any investigating accountants. Unless the target's management can explain fluctuations in ways which stand up to examination and are capable of corroboration, fundamental doubts must remain about the quality of earnings no matter what other work has been done.

A buyer is however not limited to looking just at the target's results. In the light of industry turnover levels and changes in the margins achieved by competitors, the target's own results could make a lot more sense. Industry information might be available from trade associations and use should be made of the accounts of individual companies which the buyer has already collected during the search for a suitable target.

Nevertheless, the investigating accountants may only be able to understand past results if they appreciate the impact of sales to and purchases from related parties. Other types of transactions to scrutinise include related party funding arrangements and finance costs, management charges and the remuneration of owner-directors.

It is vital to identify all related party transactions and not only because purchases may need re-sourcing and customers replacing after an acquisition. Where the prices and terms of the transactions have been abnormal then they will have confused the operating performance reported in the past. The past is also unlikely to be an adequate guide to a future in which, under new ownership, the target will no longer be related to the businesses with which it previously traded other than on an arm's length basis. It is to a further examination of future operating prospects that we now turn.

15.5 FUTURE PROSPECTS

In performing the pre-purchase review and purchase investigation, it is important for the investigating accountants to highlight matters which will be relevant to the future operating performance of the target. These matters should be reported to the potential buyer because of the effect that they could have on both the supposed fit of the target with the acquisition profile and the valuation of the target business. Always of relevance are the effects on the target's future earnings of changes in accounting policies introduced by the buyer and the scope for increased volumes of business and reduced costs after an acquisition.

Otherwise, as with the interpretation of reported results, the selection of issues requiring attention must suit the particular circumstances of a proposed acquisition. We will review eight possible areas of high risk where clues for the future may be sought.

1. Industry trends
2. Marketing
3. Regulatory requirements
4. Overseas operations
5. Fixed assets
6. Research and development
7. Reporting systems
8. Personnel

15.6 COPING WITH THE WORLD OUTSIDE

Information on the level of competition in the target's sector, current industry margins and ease of entry into the market will alert potential buyers to the vulnerability of any plans they have for the future. Further information on rates of insolvency, divestiture and growth in the industry will heighten the buyer's appreciation of the riskiness of the acquisition.

It is important to identify keys to the company's success in its markets, in particular the relative emphasis placed on price, design, reliability, technical innovation and after-sales support and the methods used to promote these aspects of the company's products and services. Only in this way can future threats to continued success begin to be identified. Distribution methods should also be described as a basis for assessing the susceptibility of the company to cost escalation and industrial action.

The impact of special regulations on the business might need to be noted because product safety and performance standards could significantly increase the cost of future product development. Regulations could have other unforeseen effects. For example, special reporting requirements, in particular for financial institutions, could result in increasingly onerous and costly obligations which the potential buyer should be aware of from the outset.

Where the target is based overseas or has significant foreign operations, the special problems associated with operating in specific political and cultural environments should also be brought to the potential buyer's attention. Management should be made aware of possible restrictions on the movement of cash and other assets, difficulties in enforcing legal contracts and threats of government intervention even to the point of expropriation.

15.7 THE INSIDE OF THE BUSINESS

The condition of fixed assets should be established. Do production facilities reflect the state of the art or, at the other extreme, are they outdated and in need of costly replacement or high and escalating expenditure on maintenance? The running down of a company's fixed asset base, by an ageing proprietor or a distant parent company, may already have been noted by the investigating accountants when interpreting the past.

Areas of current research and development activity and future commitment should be understood in terms of their likely impact on performance and liquidity. Allowance should be made where it is difficult to estimate the total cost of research and development projects. The level of research and development effort should also be compared to industry norms in order to identify future likely drains on resources and past neglect.

Manual and EDP systems for internal and external reporting should be reviewed. The extent to which the target's systems have been developed on a planned as opposed to an ad hoc basis may prove a useful guide to the strength and reliability of overall financial control and reporting. More importantly, the adequacy of the target's systems in terms of the acquiring company's future plans should be considered. Deficiencies could result in significant additional costs to the purchaser. It is particularly important to be critical when looking at expensive but perhaps inflexible and undersized computer systems.

The likely individual employee responses and union reactions to a potential acquisition and subsequent changes in management style need to be considered. In addition, the numbers of days lost through disputes, absenteeism and illness should be analysed together with union membership numbers, remuneration levels and promotion patterns. These should all be compared with the buyer's own employment record in order to determine the likelihood of a costly post-acquisition "culture shock".

Lastly, in the area of personnel, the management structure will need to be documented. Factors to pay attention to include age, length of service, succession arrangements, reporting responsibilities and the breadth of management skills and qualifications. Age and length of service will be relevant not only in assessing the strength of management but also in envisaging possible resistance to change, the scope for offering early retirement and the compensation liabilities that would arise on any redundancies. Nevertheless, it is important to identify managers whose continued employment would be fundamental to a successful acquisition and to consider what would have to be done to ensure that they did stay.

15.8 REAL SURPRISES

We have referred to many of the troubles which can await an innocent purchaser and mean that operating performance in the future will be poorer than in the past. We mentioned, for example, neglect of fixed asset replacement and research and development, the discontinuance of special trading terms with related parties and inflexible information systems.

Troubles of this type are rooted in the day-to-day operations of the business and their effects would be felt in the deteriorating results of the target. Although risks in such areas can be covered by warranties, as matters affecting operating profit, they need to be recognised mainly in valuing the target business and in drawing up post-acquisition plans.

There are however other problems which could have a sudden, serious and devastating impact on the target business or the buyer. Such problems are unlikely to be dealt with adequately through adjustment of the consideration and operational measures in the aftermath of the acquisition. Unless they wipe out the possibility of an acquisition altogether, they will probably be addressed primarily by seeking legal protection.

At an operational level, a highly profitable target needs to be handled very delicately. Because of the publicity that surrounds an acquisition, key suppliers and customers or potential competitors may come to appreciate, for the first time, the true profitability of the business which is for sale. Overnight, that profitability could evaporate. The buyer may just see a good prospective deal disappear or, alternatively, if the deal has been done, a new acquisition may suddenly look very expensive. Discretion as well as caution is important and a private buyer will have a competitive advantage over public rivals in this respect.

Catastrophes can also often occur in complex legal areas and we will look at such non-operational matters in the next two chapters under the headings of employment and legal hazards and tax skeletons. Although management may feel uneasy about handling such difficulties they should remember that most legal problems and all tax skeletons relate only to the acquisition of a company rather than business assets. This is because it is companies which cannot shake off their pre-acquisition past. Therefore, most non-operational problems can, if necessary, be avoided by making an asset purchase.

16.

EMPLOYMENT AND LEGAL HAZARDS

16.1 AREAS FOR ATTENTION

This chapter outlines the principal employment and legal hazards of buying a business either by taking a controlling interest in the shares of a company or by purchasing assets from a company, a sole trader or a partnership.

The employment liabilities which we discuss come from two main sources and they relate equally to share and asset purchases.

1. Contracts of employment
2. Pensions

The other legal problems which we present are all relevant to purchases of shares although the issue of title is also relevant when assets are bought.

3. Litigation
4. Title
5. The target's constitution
6. Contractual obligations

A buyer needs to assign clear and appropriate responsibilities in these areas to investigating accountants, solicitors, actuaries and other professionals.

16.2 CONTRACTS OF EMPLOYMENT

Where an acquisition is effected by a share purchase, there is usually no impact on contracts of employment between the target company and its employees. However, in some cases the target's management could have introduced terms into their contracts of employment which give them rights, say to leave on short notice, should their company be acquired. At the extreme, the target management may have inserted compensation provisions covering the possibility of them leaving following an acquisition, but the validity of such provisions must be open to doubt.

Buyers and their professional advisers need to make sure that they determine the extent of the buyer's obligations by obtaining details of all terms of employment including service contracts, duties, remuneration, holiday entitlements, pay review dates and periods of notice. They should also identify non-contractual but customary items such as bonuses, staff discounts and high discretionary payments on redundancy which the buyer would have to maintain after buying the target business. The length of each employee's continuous employment with the company is also important, for it would be relevant in calculating statutory redundancy payments, dismissal compensation and minimum notice.

Matters are little different when it is business assets that are bought rather than a company. In substance, the buyer takes over the contractual responsibilities of the seller and therefore must be just as meticulous in establishing the extent of the obligations that are involved. Great care is needed if redundancies are planned and it is intended that the cost should fall on the seller. If the matter is badly handled, there is a severe risk that either the seller or the purchaser could pay out redundancy money without being able to reclaim the government's normal contribution.

Identifying the employees who are actually transferred when a purchase of assets occurs can also be problematic. Strictly, the buyer takes over the contracts of all employees working in the acquired business whose employment would be terminated by the seller as a result of the sale of that business. Only the seller is in a proper position to identify the people concerned.

The careful identification of the contracts of employment taken over, whether by share or asset purchase, will assist the buyer in avoiding unexpected liabilities although specific specialist advice should be sought. We point out the sorts of liability which could arise.

Redundancy liabilities for pre-acquisition service may crystallise if a buyer sheds labour in order to realise the opportunities of an acquisition. It is particularly important for the buyer to cost the redundancies which are implicit in any post-acquisition plans. If high discretionary payments have been paid in the past, the cost can be prohibitive.

Thought should also be given to rights of compensation that the target's employees may have. Such rights could be triggered if the buyer pushes through plans to alter job descriptions, salaries, benefits or promotion structures. Unexpected compensation liabilities can arise because any substantial and detrimental change in an employee's working conditions may be treated as a case of constructive and, on the face of it, unfair dismissal.

Finally, a buyer should look out for liabilities that will become payable to the target's management under service contracts in the event of their departure.

16.3 TYPES OF PENSION SCHEME

The assets and liabilities of a company pension scheme are usually held outside the company itself. Although a company may in the future derive benefit or incur a liability as a result of a scheme's financial position, only now are such assets and liabilities starting to be reflected in companies' accounts. This is as a consequence of UK Statement of Standard Accounting Practice No.24. Consequently, buyers need to be on their guard. To appreciate the risks, it is fundamental to understand the differences between the two principal types of pension scheme, namely, the defined-contribution scheme and the defined-benefit scheme.

On retirement, the individual members of a defined-contribution or "money purchase" scheme are entitled to whatever pension can be bought with the funds contributed by themselves and, on their behalf, by the employer. Hence the liabilities of such a scheme cannot exceed its assets. The risk to a potential buyer is low if the target has a defined-contribution scheme and all liabilities to date for the employer's contributions have been recognised in the accounts. The buyer of such a business knows that, at the date of purchase, there can be no accrued but unfunded liabilities which might have to be made good later.

The issues are not so straightforward with a defined-benefit or "final salary" scheme. On retirement, individual members will receive in pension a predetermined fraction of their final salary for each year's service. To calculate the total pensions to be paid in the future, estimates are required of future wage inflation and employees' likely length of service, promotion patterns and mortality. The determination of adequate contribution levels to fund uncertain future pension costs is the specialised and speculative occupation of the actuary.

If a target business has a defined-benefit scheme, the buyer should realise that there may be accrued but unfunded liabilities at the date of purchase. In other words, the funds paid over to the scheme so far may be insufficient to provide the pensions which people have been promised and which they have earned based on their service to date.

A seller might try to reassure a buyer by stating that, at the acquisition date and on a "discontinuance basis", the target's defined-benefit scheme is fully-funded. What this means is that if everyone retired on the acquisition date then the fund could afford to pay pensions based on service to date and acquisition date salary levels. However, the actual future cost of pensions based on service to date will rise as final salaries rise so that, even in the case of a fund which is fully-funded on a discontinuance basis, the buyer may still have to meet an unfunded obligation relating to pre-acquisition service.

16.4 DEALING WITH PENSIONS

In view of the potential pitfalls, an outline agreement on pension matters should be sought as soon as possible. When it is felt that underfunding could exist, a safe solution is for the potential buyer to seek a commitment from the vendor to make whatever "top-up" payment is required to fund accrued benefits based on final salary projections rather than current salaries. Rarely if ever can a buyer rely on the results of the regular actuarial reviews performed to assist in the setting of contribution rates. An appropriate top-up payment is usually specifically calculated by an independent actuary. As an actuary's findings are unlikely to be available before the completion of the purchase agreement, a purchaser should also request that interest be paid on the final top-up payment.

It should not be forgotten that defined-benefit pension schemes are sometimes significantly overfunded. This is quite common in businesses which have made major redundancies in recent years. Redundancies arrest the growth of future pension liabilities for past service but do not themselves affect the assets available to fund those benefits.

Where there is a surplus in the scheme, a buyer will not want to draw too much attention to the issue of pensions. After an acquisition it may be possible for a buyer to improve the target's profitability if past contributions have been higher than those which are needed to fund the scheme on a continuing basis. Alternatively, if the buyer has an underfunded scheme, this could be merged with the target's. As a last resort, the surplus assets of the overfunded scheme could be repaid to the target although such repayments are currently subject to tax at 40 per cent.

So far, we have asumed that the target's pension scheme is at least clearly identifiable, but this is sometimes not the case if the target's employees have been members of a large group scheme. When the target's employees have participated in a wider defined-benefit pension scheme, the buyer must ensure that adequate "transfer payments" are made by that scheme to allow the buyer to fund the pension liabilities relating to the target's employees. It is essential that an agreed actuarial basis for the calculation of transfer payments is settled at an early stage.

The most sensitive area in the calculation will concern the sharing of any perceived surplus or underfunding in the group scheme.

An additional point to note is that pension fund trust deeds often dictate the basis on which the trustees of a fund can make transfer payments. The basis specified in the trust deed could be inadequate in the view of the buyer's actuaries. The buyer should negotiate hard to make sure that the seller bears the costs of any payments in excess of those allowed in the trust deed.

Professional advisers should also be requested to review the trust deed and rules of each of the target's pension schemes. Of particular interest are the provisions for making changes to the scheme or winding it up and any measures that have been introduced to protect a surplus from being used by a buyer.

The overriding message is to address the issues early. Pension matters are complex and the information provided by targets is often either out of date or incomplete. Consequently, pensions can be a source of considerable irritation, frustration and danger at the last minute of a negotiation. It is sobering to think that the accrued pension entitlements of a target's employees frequently exceed the amount paid for the target itself: buyers must ensure that such entitlements are properly funded.

16.5 LITIGATION

The purchaser of a company runs the risk of inheriting uninsured liabilities under legal disputes. The types of possible disputes are numerous but they include industrial accident claims, product liability suits, violations of patents, trademarks or copyrights and even violations of international trading agreements.

The buyer's professional advisers should always review a target company's procedures for identifying, reporting and progressing litigation matters. This will enable them to evaluate the risk that legal problems either will not be known about or will not be vigorously pursued by the target's management. In addition, target management should be questioned directly about whether major litigation is in progress or in prospect. Finally, when conducting an acquisition audit, the investigating accountants should seek written confirmation from solicitors used by the target as to the existence and extent of any outstanding matters being handled by them.

16.6 TITLE

The question of title concerns the seller's right to sell. Important issues need to be addressed whether the intention is to buy a limited company or merely to buy business assets. Even if a purchaser can subsequently win a case of contested title and avoid the nightmare of having completely wasted the purchase consideration, the costs involved could still be crippling. As in all the major risk areas we are discussing, it is far more cost-effective and business-like to do proper homework before an acquisition than to skimp at that stage and rely on post-acquisition litigation.

Where the seller is selling shares in a company, it is necessary to ensure that the company owns the assets used in the target business and that the seller owns the shares. Where the seller is selling the assets used in the target business, the seller's title to those assets must be verified. Much of the work in this area is performed by professional lawyers working independently of the investigating accountants. As always, it is important to avoid duplication of effort and any confusion which could mean that important procedures are simply not performed.

When verifying title to shares, a lawyer may start with the target company's founding documents, the memorandum and articles of association. These documents identify the people who subscribed for the original shares in the company. From here, the lawyer can trace the validity of the transactions which culminated in the ownership of the shares by the seller of the business. This tracing process involves the extensive use of the target company's "statutory books", the administrative histories that must be maintained by each company to comply with company legislation.

For recently formed businesses, the work we have outlined is quite likely to be performed, whereas for long-established companies, it is not customary. It may not even be strictly necessary. In the absence of suspicious circumstances, the "register of members", which forms part of the statutory books, is adequate evidence of the ownership of a company. However, if there have been known transactions in the shares of the target company within, say, the last five years, it is still wise to check that these have been properly documented. Finally, a purchase agreement for shares should contain covenants by the sellers as to their ownership and protection for the buyer by way of warranties.

Turning to assets, there are two methods which can be adopted in relation to the land held by a target or selling company. The seller's solicitors can give a "certificate of title" in terms to be agreed with the purchaser, or alternatively, the purchaser can decide to investigate title independently. If the value of land is very significant to the total value of the target business, an independent investigation is to be preferred. Where, by contrast, the land is held on leasehold at a market rental and alternative premises are available if necessary, a certificate of title should suffice.

In the case of an independent search, local authority and land charges registry searches are normally made. Where registered land is involved, vendor co-operation should be sought to perform land registry searches. One point to note is that although the searches formally protect a purchaser of land, they do not protect a purchaser of shares in a company owning land. If land is so important that full protection is needed, arrangements should be made for it to be separately purchased.

Title to other assets can be established by normal audit-type work by the investigating accountants although it may be preferable to involve solicitors. It certainly requires specialist skills to establish title in the case of intangibles such as copyrights, trademarks, designs or patents. It is also essential to conduct a search of a target or selling company's files at Companies House to reveal any registered charges. For example, assets which are to be acquired could be used to secure existing bank borrowings. Such charges should be released prior to a deal.

16.7 THE TARGET'S CONSTITUTION

A buyer should be aware of how, from a legal standpoint, a target company can be managed. It would be unfortunate if the buyers were only to discover limitations on their powers after an acquisition had been effected. Such limitations are most likely to cause a serious risk when not all the shares of a target are to be bought.

There are two points of reference for enquiries about how a target can be run. The target company's memorandum and articles of association set out the pre-emption and other rights attaching to shares, any restrictions on share transfers, the powers of directors and procedures for appointing and removing directors. In addition, there is the law relating to minority shareholders. There is a general principle, established in the case of Foss v Harbottle, that the majority governs a company. However, subsequent provisions in successive Companies Acts have established specific minority rights. Detailed consideration of rights established in a target company and in statute may spell the end of proposals to allow a minority shareholder to remain.

16.8 CONTRACTUAL OBLIGATIONS

Contractual obligations which are inherited in a company purchase may significantly constrain a target's future operations. Examples include onerous and inflexible purchase or sale contracts, leasing agreements, joint ventures, non-competition arrangements or conditions imposed by government loan or grant-making bodies.

Such commitments should be identified by the investigating accountants. Nonetheless, it is important for major contractual obligations to be reviewed in detail by the buyer's legal advisers and dealt with, where appropriate, through warranties and indemnities built into the purchase agreement. Amongst other things, the legal advisers need to establish whether there are any clauses allowing another party to terminate or modify a contract upon a change of control or whether there have been any breaches of material contracts.

17.

TAX SKELETONS

17.1 APPRECIATING THE BACKGROUND

By tax skeletons we refer to the unusual liabilities for taxation which the buyer of a company, but not the buyer of business assets, can inadvertently assume. When a target company is acquired through a share purchase, the whole of the target company's tax history comes with it. Where a company has failed to make proper tax returns, not only does unpaid tax have to be paid, but interest and penalties can be levied as well.

The risks from history which we examine in this chapter relate primarily to corporation tax. The corporation tax issues are dealt with under the following headings.

1. Understated profits
2. Distributions to shareholders
3. Chargeable gains
4. Group loss relief

In addition, we consider value added tax (VAT) and import duty, and the payroll taxes, pay-as-you-earn (PAYE) and employer and employee national insurance contributions (NIC).

In order to get a feel for possible problems, the investigating accountants need to hold detailed discussions with the target company's tax advisers and accounting personnel and they also need to review correspondence between the target company and the Inland Revenue. These exercises could reveal conditions which the Inland Revenue had specified in relation to the tax treatment of previous reorganisations and demerger transactions involving the target company. Serious tax consequences could follow if the proposed acquisition was to be effected in a way which ignored conditions set previously by the Inland Revenue.

Nevertheless, the primary purpose of the discussions and review of correspondence is to find out whether the computations of liabilities for all financial years up to the present are agreed by the Inland Revenue, submitted but subject to query, or else still in course of preparation. This exercise is important because it enables the buyer to assess the extent to which there are as yet undetermined tax liabilities or losses which can be used to reduce future tax liabilities. Failure to submit and agree computations on a prompt basis may also be symptomatic of other tax-related problems.

In addition, it is advisable, subject to the consent of the target's tax advisers, to review the last agreed corporation tax computations and any subsequent submitted or draft computations. The purpose of this review is not only to identify risk areas. It should also facilitate a better overall understanding of a company's tax affairs including the effects of previous tax planning and, where the target is a subsidiary, its relationship with the rest of its group.

Another useful way to improve understanding of the target company's tax position is to "rationalise" the tax charge for recent years. Such a rationalisation involves explaining the difference between the taxation charge shown in the accounts and that indicated by applying the prevailing corporation tax rate to the profit before tax which is shown in the accounts. Explanation of the difference serves to focus attention on material points in the company's tax computations.

Outstanding questions from the Inspector of Taxes and the subject matter of any major correspondence in the past are also of interest. They may give clues to any unrecognised liabilities for outstanding years and they may indicate possible grounds for reassessing previously agreed years.

17.2 UNDERSTATED PROFITS

Certain areas of a tax-sensitive nature should be enquired into even if there has been no apparent concern expressed by the Inland Revenue. The areas involved depend on the risks associated with specific businesses but could include the four areas specified below, all of which relate to the problems of understating taxable profits or overstating losses. In the latter case, the losses are usually described as being "tainted".

The first area for automatic enquiry would be related party sales and purchases. Uncommercial prices and terms can be used to shift taxable profits between companies and countries.

Secondly, the investigating accountant should be looking out for the "prudent" understatement of taxable profits. This could be evidenced by excessive conservatism in the determination of provisions against stocks and debtors and inadequate support for the classification of these provisions as specific deductible items for tax purposes.

Third comes a danger that is particularly relevant to the smaller family business. A target company may have reduced taxable profits or increased tax losses by incorrectly deducting personal expenses of directors and other disallowable expenditure. Current Inland Revenue practice in relation to expenditure which has been fraudulently deducted is to recover, at the very least, the full amount of that expenditure in tax, penalties and interest.

The fourth risk also relates primarily to family companies. Certain transactions, notably sales, may not be recorded in the books of account. This is a potentially serious problem in cash-based businesses and might be signalled by margins which show marked and unexplained fluctuations or which are untypical of the target's industry. Alternatively, the directors' lifestyles may appear inconsistent with the target's stated profits and the directors' disclosed remuneration.

A further clue to the possible incompleteness of the books is the presence in the annual accounts of a so-called "small company audit qualification". Auditors use this qualification in their report when they can only rely on directors' representations in certain areas and cannot obtain adequate independent evidence to establish that the accounts give a true and fair view.

It should be realised that in cases where taxable profits have been misstated because of "neglect", the time limit for re-opening assessments is generally six years. In a case of fraudulent misstatement, no time limits restrict the Inland Revenue's ability to reassess prior periods. Furthermore, the investigations involved in "back duty cases", where previous years are reassessed, are very costly and time-consuming.

17.3 DISTRIBUTIONS TO SHAREHOLDERS

When a company makes distributions by way of a dividend, it makes a payment of advance corporation tax (ACT) to the government. The ACT rate is set so that the value of ACT as a percentage of a dividend plus the related ACT is equal to the basic rate of income tax; consequently, the ACT rate is 25/75 when the basic rate of income tax is 25 per cent. Subject to certain restrictions, an ACT payment can be offset against the corporation tax, if any, due on a company's profits.

There are additional special distribution rules for so-called "close companies". The definition of close companies is a complex matter, but they include most private companies and those public companies where less than 35 per cent of the shares are held by "the public". For close companies, tax may be payable not only on actual distributions by way of dividend but also on other transactions. There is a risk that, after the acquisition of a close company, the Inland Revenue might identify distributions on which they will demand payment of tax from an unsuspecting buyer.

Benefits-in-kind provided for shareholders who are not directors can be subject to ACT. Loans made by the company can be taxed at the ACT rate where they are made to "participators", people who are typically shareholders or directors. In the latter case, the tax cannot even be offset against the paying company's mainstream corporation tax liability and is only recoverable when the loans are repaid.

Specific ACT-related risks can arise because of the special rules applying to groups of companies. Suppose the target company is more than 50 per cent owned by a parent company to which it has in the past paid dividends. ACT would not have been payable on such dividends if both companies had filed a "group income election" with the Inland Revenue. However, if ACT has not been paid and there is no group income election in force, then an unsuspecting purchaser could be faced with a bill for ACT from the Inland Revenue.

A further ACT danger can arise when the target is a member of a group. A holding company can pass on to subsidiaries in which it owns 50 per cent or more of the shares the benefit of any ACT it has paid on dividends to outside shareholders. Such a subsidiary can use this "surrendered ACT" to reduce its own liability to mainstream corporation tax.

However, surrendered ACT can only be used by a target company whilst it is in its original group. As soon the company is bought out of a group, any surrendered ACT becomes worthless. Therefore, if a target company's surplus ACT is to be paid for, it must be confirmed that the ACT was actually paid by the target.

17.4 CHARGEABLE GAINS

Chargeable gains are calculated by reference to the difference between the sales proceeds of a capital item and an adjusted original cost, the "base cost". This cost reflects the March 1982 value of an asset acquired before that date and allows for the effect of inflation experienced while holding an asset after March 1982. Two simple reliefs from paying corporation tax on chargeable gains can however cause problems for a subsequent buyer of a company.

The first relief to be wary of is rollover relief. When a company makes chargeable gains on the sale of certain capital assets, it can defer the related tax liability by deducting the gains from the base cost of new assets acquired in the previous twelve months or the subsequent three years. Rollover relief can also apply within a group, with one subsidiary rolling over a gain against new assets acquired by another subsidiary.

As a result of rollover relief, when the new assets in question are sold there is a larger than expected tax liability on the resulting gains because the base cost has been reduced. This presents a serious problem if the purchaser plans to have the target sell some fixed assets, perhaps to assist in financing the acquisition. The investigating accountants therefore need to establish the tax base costs of fixed assets. These costs may be well below their actual original costs as shown in the accounts of the target company.

The second relief that might cause problems arises under Section 273 of the Capital Gains Tax Act of 1979. Capital assets are deemed to be transferred at a value which gives rise to neither a gain nor a loss when they are transferred within a "capital gains group". Subject to recent anti-avoidance measures, this has been a group in which each company is at least 75 per cent owned by its immediate parent.

Under Section 278, when a company leaves a capital gains group, the company itself is deemed to sell and reacquire any capital asset transferred from another group company during the preceding six years. The deemed sale is effected at the asset's market value at the time of the transfer. Significant tax liabilities can result and, since the gain is seen as arising at the time of the original transfer, it may be too late to make certain elections to limit the extent of the liabilities. Therefore, the investigating accountants definitely need to identify the gains that will be deemed to arise when a target company leaves a group.

17.5 GROUP LOSS RELIEF

We complete our review of corporation tax risks by looking at another form of relief which is relevant to members of groups. This time the relief relates to trading not capital profits. Suppose that there is a company which makes taxable trading losses in a group which comprises a holding company and subsidiaries in which its direct and indirect holdings amount to 75 per cent or more. The loss-maker can surrender the losses it incurs in a period to another group company. The recipient can then offset these losses against its own taxable trading profits of the same period and so reduce its corporation tax liability.

There are risks to the buyer of a company which has supposedly either given or received the benefit of tax losses by means of group relief. The group relief claims themselves may not have been agreed with the Inland Revenue because, for instance, the giving or receiving company's tax computations have not been agreed or the claims themselves have not been properly made. Alternatively, group relief may not be available because of the application of certain wide-ranging anti-avoidance legislation. This legislation requires that particular care is exercised by the seller and the target in the year of sale.

17.6 VAT AND IMPORT DUTY

The target company's compliance with VAT legislation should be examined by the investigating accountants, especially in view of the complexity of the rules and the increasing vigilance of Customs and Excise in raising assessments for underpaid VAT. Furthermore, stiff penalties can be applied for incorrect or delayed VAT reporting. A useful starting point is to ascertain the frequency of visits by Customs and Excise personnel and to identify any material settlements or changes in practice arising from these "control visits". If control visits have been performed regularly, if the visits' results have been taken to heart and if normal VAT payments have been made promptly, then the exposure to a buyer is unlikely to be great.

Smaller and perhaps cash-based family businesses do however present special VAT risks. Personal expenditure and unrecorded transactions will have VAT consequences as well as the corporation tax consequences which we have already considered. By overstating business expenses or by not recording all sales, the target may have underdeclared its value added and hence its tax liability on that value.

There is also an additional significant VAT risk, the so-called "partial exemption problem", which can affect many types of organisation. Companies which make some sales that are exempt from VAT, as opposed to being subject to VAT at a zero rate, should not reclaim VAT on a portion of their purchases. To the extent that such VAT has been wrongly reclaimed, a company can have a significant unrecorded VAT liability.

Special risks arise in businesses with significant imports. VAT and customs duty are payable at the time of importation except where a company has a deferment arrangement. Such an arrangement is backed up by a guarantee, usually from the company's bankers. It is important that the liability for import VAT and customs duty is properly recognised in the target's accounts. In addition, the target company should-not have been reclaiming import VAT through its VAT returns without first having the certificates to prove that the VAT has been paid.

The amount of duty payable on imports is also an easily overlooked but potentially dangerous area. The valuation and classification of goods for duty purposes and the operation of quota exemptions or anti-dumping provisions are not straightforward. Disputes with the authorities could take a long time to resolve and their resolution could apply retrospectively and also have a significant effect on a target's future profitability.

Finally, companies which import goods and either export them again or put them to some qualifying use may be relieved from paying duty. All types of relief require an authorisation from the authorities and a company may also have agreed certain procedures with the authorities for handling imported goods and providing documentation. If a business is transferred into a new company, past authorisations and procedural arrangements are not automatically transferred. A buyer needs to plan the transfer so that there are no adverse effects on the business, its profitability or its cashflow.

17.7 PAYE AND NIC

It is not unknown for a target company to turn into a nightmare shortly after acquisition because of the findings of an Inland Revenue PAYE audit. It might be discovered, for example, that payments have been made to employees or casual workers without deduction of tax but that the company has no proof of its right not to deduct PAYE and NIC at source and pay these over to the Inland Revenue. Furthermore, expense allowances or benefits-in-kind may have been provided for staff without being reported to the Inland Revenue as emoluments. As a final example, payments may have been made to subcontractors without adequate proof of their self-employed status and hence, once again, without proper authority for the non-deduction of tax.

The effect of PAYE and NIC violations can be highly material when assessments are issued by the Inland Revenue to recover six years' estimated deductions. The investigating accoutant must look for material assessments issued as a result of past PAYE audits and must also have the skills and judgement to assess the materiality of any assessment that could arise because of a failure to comply with proper PAYE procedures. It can come as a great shock to the buyer of a target company with significant trading and capital losses, to be faced with a one-off PAYE and NIC liability which can in no way be mitigated or deferred.

18.

BUYING IN PUBLIC

18.1 TYPES OF REGULATION

The management of a company wanting to make an acquisition have to be aware of and comply with securities market regulations if either their own company is quoted or if the target company is quoted. In addition, management should bear in mind certain practical features of public acquisitions. They should be especially wary of becoming "carried away" and spending in excess of their own valuation of the target because they fear losing face. Management are more likely to meet determined opposition to the acquisition of a quoted company from the target's management and shareholders, a rival or a wider public.

When the buyer is quoted on The Stock Exchange, management must comply with the requirements of The Stock Exchange's rule book "Admission of Securities to Listing", the so-called "Yellow Book". The Yellow Book protects the buyer's own shareholders and the investing public and key provisions have statutory backing, notably the "listing particulars" or prospectus requirements which reflect EEC directives.

When the target is, or has recently been, a public company, then the buying company's management will have to comply with "The City Code on Take-overs and Mergers" for the protection of their own shareholders and the target's shareholders. As well as administering the City Code, the Panel on Take-overs and Mergers also administers a second set of regulations, "The Rules Governing Substantial Acquisitions of Shares".

18.2 YELLOW BOOK CLASSIFICATIONS

Acquisitions and disposals by listed and USM companies are categorised into five types: Class 1, 2, 3 and 4 transactions and "reverse takeovers". We will describe the classification criteria as they relate to acquisitions. For a public buyer, post-acquisition transactions, such as the disposal of unwanted parts of a target business, could also fall within the classification criteria outlined. The criteria will also apply to a listed or USM seller and could in this way come to affect an unsuspecting private company buyer.

A Class 1 transaction arises where any one of a series of four comparisons between the target and the buyer gives an answer of 15 per cent or more for a listed company or 25 per cent or more for a USM company. The comparisons are to be made between the following pairs of values.

1. The net assets of the target and the buyer
2. The pre-tax profits of the target and the buyer
3. The consideration and the net assets of the buyer
4. Any shares issued by the buyer to make an acquisition and the buyer's existing equity

The other classifications apply equally to listed and USM companies. A Class 2 transaction is a transaction which does not fall into Class 1 but for which one or more of the four comparisons gives an answer of five per cent or more.

A Class 3 transaction is one in which all four comparisons give answers of less than five per cent.

A Class 4 transaction occurs where the target is owned by a related party. For example, a Class 4 situation arises when assets or shares are to be purchased from a current or recent director or substantial shareholder of the buying company or one of its subsidiaries, or from anyone else associated with such a person. Class 4 transactions can equally involve sales to such related parties, notably in the case of a management buy-out from a quoted company.

A very substantial acquisition or reverse takeover occurs where the comparisons referred to for Class 1, 2 and 3 transactions would yield answers of 100 per cent or more. A reverse takeover also occurs in other circumstances which would result in the sellers of the acquired business receiving shares which would allow them to take control of the buyer.

We will look shortly at the requirements relating to each type of transaction. In broad terms, these requirements follow the principle that the more material a transaction is to the interests of the existing shareholders, the greater must be their involvement in the acquisition either by being provided with more information or by having the deal put to them for approval.

It should be remembered that the requirements we will identify for different types of acquisition are quite independent of the normal requirements relating to the share and debt issues which may be integral to an acquisition. Any share issue which would increase the number of shares of a particular class by 10 per cent or more and any debt issue will trigger a need for so-called "listing particulars" to be submitted to The Stock Exchange and circulated through the Extel Statistical Services. In the case of a Class 1 transaction, the listing particulars must also be sent to shareholders.

Listing particulars generally include the information required in a prospectus. They comprise details of the securities offered and information on the issuer's activities, management, development and prospects. In the case of a share issue, the last five years' accounts will also be needed although this requirement will be reduced to two years in the case of a debt issue.

18.3 CLASS 1, 2 AND 3 REQUIREMENTS

In the case of a Class 1 transaction, a circular must be sent to the buying company's shareholders. The circular would contain information about the transaction and details about the target business of the same sort as would appear in a prospectus about that business if it was applying for admission to listing. In particular, the buyer's plans for the future development of the target should be indicated. Also included in the circular would be information about the buying company or group and both the buyer's and the target's borrowings. There would be details of material contracts relating to the acquisition and of directors' share interests in the buying company.

An accountants' report on the target company is required and this is usually prepared by the auditors of the buyer. The report typically contains balance sheets and profit and loss accounts for the preceding five years and statements of source and application of funds for the preceding three years, together with a full set of notes and disclosures. The reporting accountants must express an opinion on the truth and fairness of the information given.

The reporting accountants are also expected to provide written comments to the buying company's directors and financial advisers on the mandatory directors' statement regarding the adequacy of their working capital in the foreseeable future. The foreseeable future is normally taken to extend one year from the acquisition date and the directors' statement on working capital needs to be supported by reasonably detailed profit and cash flow forecasts which the reporting accountants should review.

Exemptions from any of the Class 1 reporting requirements are pragmatic. For example, no accountants' report is required where a listed company is being acquired since the relevant information is already publicly available.

The Quotations Department of The Stock Exchange should be consulted through the buyer's stockbrokers where it is particularly onerous to report on five years' profit and loss accounts. This can occur whenever an entity other than a limited company is being acquired. For example, divisional management accounts could constitute the only relevant financial information and this information is unlikely to have been prepared to publication standards. In such circumstances, the Quotations Department may sanction the reporting of information for a shorter period than five years.

Where any of the four comparisons referred to previously highlights a relationship of 25 per cent or more and the buyer is a listed company, not a USM company, the transaction constitutes a major Class 1 transaction and must be approved by the buyer's shareholders prior to its completion. Shareholders' approval may also be required where the accountants' report in a circular does not contain an unqualified or "clean" audit opinion on the five years' accounts of the target.

A further requirement is that for any proposed Class 1 transaction, the buying company has to send an immediate announcement to The Stock Exchange's Company Announcements Office giving particulars of the business being acquired, its assets and pre-tax profits. The announcement will also contain details of the consideration, the service contracts to be offered to any new directors and the benefits expected to arise from the acquisition.

The only fixed requirement for a Class 2 transaction is that an announcement must be made along the same lines as for a Class 1 transaction. With a Class 3 transaction, an announcement only needs to be made where the consideration is being satisfied by an issue of shares. Both Class 2 and Class 3 transactions can be upgraded to Class 1 and Class 2 respectively where they can be aggregated with a series of similar transactions occurring in a period since the last accounts.

18.4 OTHER YELLOW BOOK REQUIREMENTS

The requirements for a Class 4 transaction are determined largely by the nature of the transaction itself. Where the transaction is also a Class 1, 2 or 3 transaction or a reverse takeover, the requirements applying to those transactions will also apply. However, the special concern of The Stock Exchange on a Class 4 acquisition is that the terms should be fair and reasonable from the point of view of the public shareholders given the fact that the transaction is with a related party.

To this end, a circular will normally be required to be sent to shareholders. This could include an accountants' report on the valuation of the assets being acquired and enough information on the acquisition to enable shareholders to form their own view on whether the transaction is in the interests of the company. The Stock Exchange will also require that the consent of the shareholders in a general meeting should be obtained and that interested directors and shareholders should not vote at such a meeting. A dispensation from the requirement for shareholder approval may be granted if the transaction is sufficiently small in value.

In general, for a Class 4 transaction it is advisable, at the earliest opportunity, to consult with the Quotations Department of The Stock Exchange in order to determine the likely extent of the requirements relating to circulars, accountants' reports and shareholder approvals. It is also a requirement of the Yellow Book that the Quotations Department is consulted before a listed company enters into any contract relating to a Class 4 transaction.

Turning to the case of a reverse takeover, the listed buyer's shares are often suspended from listing until the shareholders have approved the acquisition and information along the lines required for new applicants for listing has been provided.

After suspension, a company's listing may be restored and it may even be restored before shareholders' approval has been obtained. This will be the case where the transaction involves businesses of similar size and activity, where the enlarged group is suitable for listing and where there will be no material change in voting control and management personnel.

Finally, before proceeding to consider the City Code, which serves to protect the shareholders of a publicly held target, we mention the Yellow Book's requirements relating to offer documents which seek to protect those same shareholders.

The over-riding principle in this area is that a document supporting a listed or USM company's offer to acquire the shares of another company should enable the target's shareholders to assess the true merits of the offer. The litany of requirements is familiar and includes five years' accounts of the offeror, information about its business, prospects and borrowings, and statements as to the adequacy of working capital and the effect of the acquisition. There will of course also be the pure technical detail concerning what is being acquired and for what consideration.

By way of additional protection to the target company's shareholders, the offer document must contain the warning that, in cases of doubt, a professional adviser should be consulted. Furthermore, all

offer documents must be vetted in advance of issue by The Stock
Exchange.

18.5 THE SPIRIT OF THE CITY CODE

All listed companies must observe the City Code. The City Code itself
applies to all acquisitions of companies with any public shareholder
involvement in the previous ten years. A principal aim of the City Code
is to ensure that a target company's shareholders are treated fairly and
equally and that the target company's board has sufficient time to set out
its views on an offer to the target's shareholders. It significantly extends
the application of statutory principles such as the prohibition of insider
dealing and the need to disclose an interest in a company's shares to the
company itself.

The City Code is administered by a non-government committee, the
Panel on Take-overs and Mergers, whose Chairman is appointed by the
Governor of the Bank of England and whose other members are either
appointed by the Governor or represent bodies whose members are
involved in acquisitions. Since its inception in 1969, the Panel has
attempted to ensure that the City's self-regulation remains credible and
is not swept away in favour of statutory measures.

Those who are authorised to carry on investment business under the
Financial Services Act 1986 are required to comply with the Code and
the rulings of the Panel or their authorisation may be withdrawn. Any-
body who is advising a buyer almost certainly needs to be authorised
under the 1986 Act. Furthermore, advisers could be required not to act
for a buyer or seller who is not complying with or who is likely not to
comply with the Code or the Panel's rulings. Effectively, non-
compliance can mean exclusion from UK securities markets.

The City Code comprises 10 general principles and 38 detailed rules.
We will briefly describe the principles and some of the most important
rules although it is important to realise that the spirit and not just the letter of the City Code must be heeded. It will therefore often be wise to
consult the Panel prior to entering into transactions in order to ascertain
how such transactions may be viewed.

The general principles require that all holders of the same class of a
target company's shares must be treated similarly by the would-be
buyer and the target's management. They must all have access to all relevant information and time to act on it. Announcements and statements
made by target and buying managements should be responsibly
researched, carefully prepared and accurate and should not be motivated by self-interest.

The target company's management must not frustrate an offer but instead, under the general principles, should allow their shareholders to determine whether the offer is in their interests. As for a would-be buyer's management, under the general principles they must not oppress a minority of the target's shareholders by, for example, obtaining control without offering fair terms for buying out other shareholders.

18.6 THE RULES OF THE CITY CODE

We turn now to some of the 38 rules. Our aim is merely to give a flavour of the rules and identify some of the pitfalls that may trouble an unwary buyer.

Under Rule 6, if an offeror buys shares at a price higher than that currently being offered to all shareholders, then it must make an immediate announcement increasing the offer price to reflect, at a minimum, the higher purchase price it has paid. The minimum offer price must also not be less than the price paid for any shares in the three months prior to the offer.

Rule 9 requires a general offer for all the target's remaining shares to be made where any party and parties acting in concert acquire 30 per cent of a target or where parties already owning between 30 and 50 per cent acquire more than an additional two per cent in a year. The general offer must include an offer to buy for cash at a price not less than the highest price paid by the offeror in the preceding 12 months.

Rule 10 states that all offers must be conditional upon 50 per cent control of the company being achieved through acceptance of the offer. This rule limits the ability of a buyer to obtain significant influence or effective control by a low-priced general offer.

Under Rule 11, any bid made by a purchaser who has bought for cash more than 15 per cent of a target's shares in the 12 months prior to the bid must also contain a cash alternative at a minimum of the highest price paid.

Rule 21 prevents a target's management from frustrating an actual or imminent bid by adopting certain defences unless these are carried out in pursuance of a previously existing contract or are approved by the target's shareholders in a general meeting. Such frustrating action includes issuing new shares, granting share options, issuing convertible loan stocks, making material disposals or acquisitions and entering into transactions not in the normal course of business.

Rule 38 was introduced to limit the actions of recognised market-makers in securities who were exempt from the Code's requirements. They could previously help a buyer or target to bypass the Code by undertaking transactions on their behalf. In general, such "helpful" transactions are prohibited and if they are entered into, the market-makers are liable to be subjected to the Code in their own right.

18.7 TIMETABLE FOR A CONTESTED BID

Contained within Rules 30 to 33 of the City Code is a timetable for the conduct of a contested bid which seeks to meet the objective that managements and shareholders should have adequate time to prepare, absorb and act on information. Some of the key dates are set out below.

Day 0   -   bidder posts offer document within 28 days of announcing an offer
Day 14   -   last day for target to issue first defence circular to share-holders
Day 21   -   earliest day for closing the first offer and, on the following day, announcing the level of acceptances
Day 39   -   last day for target to issue final defence material including details of forecast profits and proposed dividends
Day 42   -   shareholders who have accepted the first offer are free to change their minds
Day 46   -   bidder revises offer for the last time and is barred for 14 days from raising its stake to more than 30 per cent
Day 60   -   declare offer unconditional or concede defeat by 5.00pm on the basis of acceptances received by 3.00pm

One event which can upset the timetable is a rival bid and this will usually lead the Panel to extend the deadlines. Alternatively, the referral of a bid to the Monopolies and Mergers Commission can interrupt the process we have outlined.

18.8 SUBSTANTIAL ACQUISITIONS RULES

In addition to the City Code, there are "The Rules Governing Substantial Acquisitions of Shares" known as the "SARs". These rules were originally introduced to deal with "dawn raids" and the difficulties they caused for targets' boards. The SARs apply to purchases of shares in UK listed companies resident in the UK and Ireland.

A dawn raid is a sudden purchase of shares as a result of which a buyer's holding in a public target is taken up to the 30 per cent holding which, under Rule 9 of the City Code, triggers a general offer. Such a burst of activity can allow a sizeable block of shares to be built up at a comparatively low premium on the previous market price prior to making an offer.

The SARs Rule 1 forbids a person or persons acting in concert from acquiring within a 7 day period 10 per cent of a company's shares so as to bring a holding up to between 15 and 30 per cent. Certain exemptions to Rule 1 are allowed in Rule 2, for example, where there is a single acquisition from a single shareholder. Rule 3 requires same day disclosure to The Stock Exchange of holdings of 15 per cent or more while Rules 4 and 5 deal with tender offers and concert parties and are of less immediate concern to us.

The regulations covering buying and selling where public companies are involved are extensive and complex. In view of the specialist nature of these regulations and their inapplicability to many readers, we have kept our discussion brief. Nevertheless, executive management of listed and USM companies contemplating acquisitions must ensure that they are familiar with the detailed regulations and that they consult fully with their stockbrokers and other professional advisers.

19.

ACQUIRING ABROAD

19.1 HOME TRUTHS

In this chapter we discuss how the familiar acquisition issues we have previously identified need extending and reinterpreting when you are buying abroad. We are not about to embark upon an international whirlwind tour. For a host of countries we could of course describe the acquisitions scene and how it is affected by economic circumstances and regulations affecting business organisation, exchange control, foreign investment, accounting and taxation. Such an approach would be subject to rapid obsolescence and, besides, no manager could or should be expected to maintain a detailed technical knowledge of acquisitions around the globe or even in one or two selected countries.

We also steer clear of advocating overseas acquisitions on the back of great trends such as globalisation, international deregulation or the Single European Market. International acquisitions are neither panaceas nor irresistible fashions. They should be justified on the same grounds as domestic acquisitions.

The approach of the Single European Market will probably promote a flurry of acquisition activity. Nevertheless, managers should identify the benefits in their own particular circumstances before joining the rush. For example, synergy gains may well be realised through European acquisitions because of the emergence of a larger market. The better exploitation of brand investment and improved economies of scale are both possibilities, but their achievement should be planned and examined before an acquisition reaches the stage of serious negotiation.

The single truly distinguishing feature of an overseas acquisition is that the target conducts its business in a foreign currency. In preparing its own accounts, the buyer translates the profits earned by the target and the net assets of the target into the buyer's own currency and this introduces a new element of variability into measurement of the buyer's performance. As the buyer's own currency strengthens, so the foreign currency profits and the value of the target are worth less and vice versa.

One way to reduce the variability is to take out borrowings denominated in the target's currency so that rises and falls in the value of the target and its profits are offset in part by rises and falls in the value of the buyer's liabilities and interest costs. The exchange risk that is associated with an overseas acquisition should be built into any assessment of how a particular acquisition will contribute towards the profitability, growth and risk objectives of a business.

19.2 UNDERSTANDING THE TARGET

Before you buy any business you should understand its environment and its previous management. When making a domestic acquisition, the main challenge is to understand the target's industry and the problems of managing in that industry. This is because it can be taken for granted that domestic buyers are familiar with the economic, political, legal and cultural background which, after all, they share with their targets. This is not true of foreign acquisitions, even in Commonwealth countries where there is a common heritage or in other EEC countries which are subject to a common process of harmonisation.

Consequently, anyone who believes that buying businesses abroad will help them to realise profitability, growth or risk objectives, should only pursue that strategy if they have done their homework on the countries involved or if they have hired people with the necessary knowledge. The costs of this extra homework and advice may be significant in the context of an acquisition and could even undermine the viability of a deal.

When considering an acquisition in another country, buyers should assess the political system, its stability and its treatment of private enterprise. Buyers should also find out about the economy and its ability to generate consumer demand and to supply labour, materials, communications and transport of suitable quality at an appropriate cost.

There are also likely to be different business practices which affect financing, legal structures, taxation and the rights of shareholders, management and employees. As a result, a target in a familiar industry may look unfamiliar. For example, the practice of financing trade debt through bills of exchange is prevalent in countries such as Spain. Obvious differences often strike a buyer during the search for a target. The quality and quantity of publicly available information may surprise a buyer who is used to the UK's audited published accounts. The mere compilation of a list of candidates may involve unexpected amounts of time, money and frustration.

Financial reporting objectives, accounting policies and accounting standards may lead to misinterpretation of the results used to assess and value a target. In some countries tax is regarded as a distribution out of profit rather than a charge against profit and it is therefore important to understand what a seller means by profit. In West Germany and Scandinavian countries allowable tax accounting rules will be reflected in the published accounts. The depreciation of fixed assets, the valuation of stocks and the recognition of liabilities can differ greatly from country to country. Surprises can occur even in sophisticated economies such as the United States where stocks may be valued on a last-in first-out basis and not on the first-in first-out basis which is normal in the UK.

19.3 MANAGING ABROAD

The success of many acquisitions depends upon the buyer's ability to manage the target after acquisition so as to improve upon previous performance or integrate the target's operations with those of the buyer. The management skills required to achieve either of these objectives may prove to be especially elusive with a foreign acquisition. Many companies follow the practice of having an expatriate general manager and financial controller. Although this aids communication with the parent company, it can cause resentment. A management team sent abroad by the buyer may find its style simply does not work in a different culture. A local management team may however be hard to motivate, monitor and control from a distant head office.

Once again, the message is clear. If you do not have the necessary experience and knowledge, then either develop it or buy it in before embarking on a strategy of foreign acquisition. The widely differing experiences of UK companies who have made acquisitions in the United States, with excellent or disastrous consequences, may be largely explained by the way they have approached the challenge of managing abroad.

Multinational accounting firms are unique amongst professional advisers in being able to provide consistent on-the-spot guidance in most countries. They should be able to give objective advice which is based upon a detailed knowledge of the opportunities and pitfalls of operating in a particular country. Most of these firms have grown their practices by following their clients as they have expanded overseas.

They should therefore be familiar with managing international mergers and acquisitions and they can be useful as a sounding board.

19.4 COMPETITION LAW

Competition law is the most obvious threat to a strategy of overseas acquisition. A few countries, notably Italy, have little legislation to enforce competition. Most countries do however have legislation and it is important to understand the following specific aspects of the target country's competition laws.

1. Optional or compulsory procedures for notifying an acquisition to the authorities before or after it happens
2. Industry, market share or size criteria used to trigger the investigation or the outright prohibition of an acquisition
3. The length of time taken to complete investigations
4. Appeal procedures and their cost, timescale and likely success
5. Provisions affecting collaborative arrangements which stop short of acquisition
6. Additional regulations relating to acquisitions by foreigners
7. Political factors which may cause an interpretation of the law to be stretched to a particular buyer's advantage or disadvantage

There may also be hidden competition law. In the United States, individual states may operate draconian anti-takeover legislation under which a change in ownership triggers onerous requirements to submit to inspection or licensing procedures.

19.5 LIQUIDITY AND DIVIDENDS

A buyer's ability to generate liquidity and dividends from an acquisition can be limited when the acquisition is made overseas. A number of issues should be considered before implementing a strategy to acquire abroad. Banking practices and the quality of the support and facilities that are available from financial institutions vary greatly from country to country.

It may be difficult to fund an acquisition abroad using the assets of the target because of limitations on a company giving financial assistance for the purchase of its own shares. Alternatively, depending upon the country, the relevant legislation could be less restrictive than in the UK.

"Thin capitalisation" provisions may limit debt to equity ratios and require investors to make a greater fixed investment than they would otherwise like in a foreign target. Distributions of profits from a foreign subsidiary may also be unattractive because of the tax that must be paid to the overseas government as a result. Indeed, an overseas subsidiary may not be able to pay dividends to the buyer because of foreign exchange controls applied by the host country.

19.6 CORPORATE CULTURE

We view corporate culture as comprising a company's image and its ways of giving its employees job satisfaction. In a domestic context, acquisitions can cause trouble in both these areas. An acquisition can damage corporate image and job satisfaction in both the buyer and the target and harmonisation can be costly. With international acquisitions, the divergence between the corporate cultures of the buyer and the target is likely to be aggravated by national and language differences.

Nevertheless, cross-border acquisitions need not be more costly and difficult than domestic acquisitions. Where the buyer and the target operate in distinct national markets, different images will not taint and confuse each other and employees are unlikely to come into contact and start making invidious comparisons. In such cases there is no need for costly harmonisation and indeed it should be positively avoided.

For example, it may be particularly dangerous to remove a local manager's minority equity stake in an overseas operation simply because the parent is used to having 100 per cent subsidiaries. This may be seen as highly demotivating.

19.7 SPOTTING THE SKELETONS

A buyer may find that a target holds a number of nasty surprises which only emerge after the purchase. With domestic acquisitions we identified the skeletons that might arise from employment matters, litigation, poor title, the target's constitution, contractual obligations and taxation. In an international setting some of these issues can call for specific care.

Any buyer contemplating an overseas turn round or takeover should be aware that employment protection legislation is particularly onerous in some European countries. This makes it difficult and expensive to rationalise a target's workforce. Pensions legislation is also a minefield for the unwary and buyers will invariably need to enlist the help of local experts or an international firm of benefit consultants. In addition, standards of business integrity should be assessed along with attitudes towards the taxation authorities. For example, although it happens on a reducing scale, separate books of account for shareholders and the taxation authorities are common in some countries. Such practices can give rise to substantial tax skeletons.

Especially in the United States, a target's constitution may contain unpleasant provisions which are triggered by an acquisition. Changes in a company's constitution are widely used by corporate managements to make themselves into highly unattractive acquisition targets. Defences known generally as "shark repellents" may make it more difficult to clear out the target's management after a takeover or they may make it necessary to obtain unusual shareholder approvals for a takeover to succeed in the first place.

Furthermore, in the United States the scale of the liability faced by a business as a result of litigation or an underinsured risk may be beyond the expectation of a UK buyer. Environmental protection laws in the United States may appear horrific from a UK perspective. In short, every country's laws are different and they will therefore generate unique risks in relation to employment, taxation and other matters which must be addressed by locally based professionals.

19.8 CLINCHING THE DEAL

A key issue in the pursuit of any acquisition strategy is to ensure that a potentially advantageous deal is not lost because negotiations reach a stalemate or because another buyer succeeds. It will be far more difficult to understand sellers and rivals when buying abroad and to appreciate how a deal can be clinched or why it should be abandoned.

A buyer should be prepared to be flexible in concluding an international deal. The UK practice of obtaining indemnities and warranties which are qualified by a disclosure letter may not be achievable. Outright acquisitions may be uncommon in a target country: they may also be inadvisable if there are significant cultural differences or if there are only a few areas with significant scope for synergy between two businesses. Gradual acquisitions, collaborative projects, joint ventures or reciprocal minority shareholdings are alternatives which are likely to require greater attention than is usual in a domestic context.

Hostile bids are virtually unknown in a variety of countries such as Japan, West Germany, the Netherlands and Spain. In attempting a contested public bid overseas, it is important from the outset to enlist local experts: they can help develop tactics to counter the target's defences and a rival bidder's moves and they can ensure compliance with legislation to protect investors. Any sort of negotiation will also call for an understanding of local ways of doing business if the seller's and buyer's actions are not to be misinterpreted by the other side.

Buyers should be aware of "accounting" advantages that they may have over foreign rivals. For example, UK buyers, like German buyers, may be able to pay a little more than American or Japanese companies because they can write off goodwill immediately on acquisition without depressing future earnings. Nevertheless, the UK buyer may be at a disadvantage along with the American through not receiving any tax relief on goodwill write-offs.

A UK public company buyer may have better access to equity funds for an acquisition compared to a foreign buyer who might be relying on junk bonds or other forms of debt. Different tax regimes may also allow a UK buyer to give a seller more without actually incurring higher costs than a rival.

Nevertheless, a UK buyer could find that tax discrimination against foreigners makes it a damaging exercise to try and outbid the local competition. Again, an issue which is fundamental to a domestic acquisition, namely sticking to a proper limit price, is of equal applicability overseas. The strangeness of the environment and the apparent glamour of an international acquisition should not blind a buyer to such unexciting truths.

20.

THE AFTERMATH

20.1 FULFILLING THE STRATEGIC PURPOSE

After an acquisition has been completed, the work begins to fulfil its strategic purpose. Only the slightest pause can be allowed for celebration and relaxation before addressing the issues of the aftermath. The responses to the issues which we will develop in this chapter are summarised in the Issues Management Guide in Appendix I.6.

In Chapter 3 we identified five basic types of acquisition which could be pursued to enhance profitability, growth or risk control. They were the asset strip, the turn round, the investment, the takeover and the merger. Management should know what sort of acquisition they intended. Nevertheless, in the case of an acquisition of a public target where there has been limited scope for investigation prior to the purchase, it is often a good idea to carry out an in-depth review of what exactly has been bought. This allows the buying management to confirm or modify the strategic purpose of the deal. All the same, this investigation should be completed as quickly as possible because the basic message for the aftermath of any acquisition is that you should get on with fulfilling the strategic purpose.

In the case of the asset strip, management should get on with the disposals and realise the profits that justified the acquisition. They should not become sentimentally attached to a business which they have already decided is strategically weak and has been badly managed.

Fulfilling the strategic purpose of an asset strip should be more straightforward than for the other sorts of acquisition. These acquisitions are characterised by a continuing interest in the target business and what binds a target business together are its people and its image.

Even in cases where some of the target's employees are considered inadequate or unnecessary and where the image needs polishing or transforming, the primary post-acquisition task is to maintain the identity and motivation of the people in the target business. The buyer's people may also need similar reassurance. If a business falls apart because people lose the desire to work well for that organisation then it will be impossible to fulfil any strategic purpose other than that of stripping the assets out of a now useless shell. In short, in discussing the aftermath of an acquisition we shall be concerned with those familiar key performance areas of corporate image and job satisfaction.

20.2 REACTIONS TO ACQUISITION

The universal reaction to an acquisition amongst employees, customers and suppliers is a feeling of uncertainty. This applies whether the buyers are familiar faces who have staged a management buy-out or a faceless and distant multinational. The uncertainty each employee feels is about their own job security, remuneration, status and prospects. It is not just poor performers who feel uncertainty, indeed they might think they have the least to fear if an acquisition gives them hope of wiping the slate clean and starting again.

Uncertainty is very damaging to a business. When employees are worried about their own future, they think less about the goals of the organisation as a whole. When employees are thinking about safety, they are less likely to be innovative and enterprising in their work.

As well as engendering uncertainty, an acquisition is likely to make people volatile and sensitive. Apparently small changes in circumstances may cause significant changes in behaviour. This may be seen in people's tendency to oscillate between looking for another job or sticking it out, and between feeling fired up by the opportunities presented by an acquisition or fed up because the acquisition appears to frustrate their ambitions. This sensitivity will display itself when the buyer's culture clashes with the old way of doing things and when intruders from the buyer's side threaten the sense of identity which people in the target have built up over the years.

20.3 COMMUNICATION AND MOTIVATION

The only way to limit the uncertainty, the volatility and the sensitivity is through communication. Communication with employees, customers and suppliers cannot start too soon or be too direct. Good communication involves telling people honestly about the buyer and the buyer's intentions and ways of doing business. It is important not to sound exultant and gloating about the acquisition and not to issue bland statements of reassurance which are bound to be met with scepticism. If credible information is not given, depressing rumours will fill the vacuum that has been left.

Credible reassurance and information are the main requirements in the investment type of acquisition, because the buyer is fundamentally satisfied with the target's business and management and does not see itself as having any useful operational contribution to make. Nevertheless, even in this case the target needs to be not just reassured and informed but also motivated and that will not be achieved by benevolent and whimsical dictatorship of any sort. Instead, in key areas of profitability, cashflow management and capital expenditure, the buyer needs to set minimum standards and challenging objectives. Performance should be monitored, achievement should be recognised and any other form of "interference" avoided. The buyer also needs to monitor performance in relation to the original justification for the acquisition and this monitoring, which should barely affect the target's management, is discussed later in the chapter.

When we move on to consider other sorts of acquisitions, buyers need to do still more. Justifications for the turn round, the takeover and the merger are rooted in the belief that the buyer can effect beneficial change.

20.4 MANAGING CHANGE POSITIVELY

Some buyers might think that change is something which has to be bludgeoned through against a fierce conservative resistance. Any attempt to bludgeon people into change will indeed probably meet conservative resistance but this is avoidable. There are alternative ways of trying to achieve change.

There are two principal types of change which may be needed following an acquisition. There is corrective change which is required to increase efficiency and focus and put a poorly managed target back on the right track, as in a turn round or a takeover. There is also the change that is involved in integrating two operations, as in a takeover or a merger, to achieve synergy.

In the rest of this section we present some of the basic principles of managing change before looking at their application to acquisitions.

1. Desirable changes will not happen on their own but have to be introduced.

2. Because change is difficult to manage, those changes which give the greatest benefit with the minimum disruption should be established as priorities.
3. Change is less likely to be resisted if there is dissatisfaction with the present state of affairs and a common desire for improvement.
4. If people are involved in discussing the way to achieve change, then both the quality of the changes and the ease of their implementation will be improved.
5. "Big bangs" rarely work and it is generally better to break a process of change into stages which people can assimilate.
6. After the introduction of change, performance can show erratic initial movements. Unsustainable improvements sometimes occur because people are stimulated by change of any sort. Alternatively, there may be deterioration in the short-term simply because people have to get used to doing things differently. Targets for improved performance should therefore not be too demanding or rigid in the early days and management should be patient in waiting for the benefits to show.
7. Changes should not be sneaked through furtively or else they will be seen as sinister. They should instead be marked by announcements, ceremonies or even celebrations.

20.5 CORRECTIVE MANAGEMENT

It is easy to see the corrective management in a turn round or takeover as an opportunity to adopt a high-handed and authoritarian approach which is totally at odds with the basic principles we have just outlined. This would be wrong.

Corrective management involves shedding inadequate and excess personnel and making tough decisions about discontinuing old practices and learning new habits. That however makes it even more important to carry the remaining people with you, otherwise they will be paralysed by uncertainty or they may cause damage by their heightened volatility and sensitivity. Initiative, retention, commitment and industrial relations will all suffer.

Furthermore, where corrective action is required, management should be prepared to find that they are pushing at an open door. If a target business has been poorly run, then people are likely to expect and even want change. Only if the initial opportunity is not taken or if people get the impression that they have no power to influence the nature of change will a defensive view emerge that everything was really fine as it was.

20.6 INTEGRATION

In a takeover or a merger the buyer anticipates achieving synergy by integrating some aspects of the buyer's and the target's operations. What we have said previously about establishing priorities clearly applies here too. Integration should only be sought in areas of real potential for synergy since it is too difficult to attempt merely for cosmetic reasons. Indeed, the integration of diverse businesses is difficult even for a company which is growing organically.

Decisive action will be needed where improved profitability is to be sought through economies of scale, whether in terms of fixed and working capital, overheads or contribution levels. For example, the streamlining of a distribution network, the rationalisation of product lines, improvements in credit control, the elimination of duplicated functions and the renegotiation of buying and selling prices will not happen on their own. In addition, if by acquisition, management have forged a business which can enter new markets, then they must positively position the business in those markets, advertise its presence and establish its credibility with potential customers.

A particular difficulty of attempting to bring about changes which will bring synergy is that the need for change will not be as apparent as in the case of correcting poor performance. Indeed, sceptics will point out that if the change is poorly managed there will be no synergy gain but a pure loss in operating performance.

Attempts to achieve integration can cover many areas, including organisation, central service functions, personnel policies, systems, physical facilities, marketing and distribution. A strict appraisal of which areas would benefit from integration should be performed before entering into a consultative process to determine how to carry through the changes. It is usual to see committees doing such work. This helps minimise the risk of excluding and alienating one side or the other. It also helps people with different company cultures to become used to working with each other and forge a new style.

There is one difficulty however that will always beset a merger exercise, no matter how carefully balanced the committees have been. One side will still be seen as being in control, perhaps because it has supplied the chief executive. Given the volatility of behaviour after an acquisition, people can latch on to such matters when they are frustrated on some small point and suddenly become disaffected and disruptive.

20.7 MONITORING AN ACQUISITION

It is important that management monitor post-acquisition performance against the original justification for an acquisition, for example by reference to the high level financial appraisal which should be performed before entering into detailed negotiations. It is by doing this that management find out if they had the understanding to identify a suitable opportunity and the skills to realise that opportunity.

If, as a consequence, the buying management realise that they cannot fulfil the strategic purpose of an acquisition then they have two options. They can buy in the necessary talent or, as a last resort, they can start trying to sell a business which they should apparently never have bought in the first place. Both courses of action are common in practice although they are usually taken belatedly. It is not unknown for managers to take credit for having "solved" post-acquisition problems in this way even though the problems were created in the first place by their own ill-conceived acquisition strategies or their own poor management of the acquisition process.

Other matters which require monitoring result from actions taken earlier in the acquisition process to address key issues. Many of the legal measures taken to deal with the risks of buying a business will have implications for post-acquisition management. For example, in earn-out deals, additional consideration is dependent upon performance after the purchase and management need to ensure that the accounting measurement of that performance is carried out in a manner which is fair, in accordance with the sale agreement and acceptable to the seller. There is often a temptation for the buyer to "go easy" in this area and pay a little over the odds so as not to sour the relationship with those sellers who are still involved with the business. This may be construed as weakness and may be met with contempt. In general, decisions to make concessions should only be taken at the highest level.

The really difficult problems of earn-out deals relate to the reluctance that both the buying and selling management may feel about taking steps which are in the long-term strategic interest of the business. It is not good enough merely to try and muddle through after an acquisition. The issues must be thought about in advance of committing yourself to an earn-out.

Management should also take full advantage of the rights of redress established at the time of the acquisition under warranties and indemnities. It will be particularly important to ensure that all claims against the seller are identified at an early stage and are properly supported by documentation. To illustrate this, if there was an indemnity given in respect of returns of faulty stock sold prior to the acquisition, then adequate, independently verifiable procedures for recording and valuing such returns would be required.

In the case of a purchase of a public company, warranties and indemnities will not have been secured at the time of the acquisition. One of the post-acquisition tasks will nevertheless be to identify areas of short-fall between the anticipated and actual worth or performance of the acquired company. A buyer may wish to disclose publicly provisions which it has had to make against the target's stocks and debtors or the extent of any unrealistic assumptions which underlay projections or forecasts made by the target at the time of the acquisition. However, management should be wary of undermining morale within the acquired business as a result of such disclosures. In addition, the large post-acquisition provisions which are attractive under acquisition accounting may strain public credibility.

The major post-acquisition risk on the tax planning front which will not be covered by way of warranty or indemnity will relate to changes in a target company's trade. The benefit of a target company's trading losses or unrelieved advance corporation tax payments can be lost if there is a major change in the nature and conduct of a target company's trade or business.

In deciding on a valuation of the target, the buyer should already have decided whether the strategic reasons for pursuing an acquisition would threaten the use of such tax assets. Nevertheless, to the extent that post-acquisition plans for the target business change, for whatever reason, the tax risks of a change in the conduct of a trade or business should be subject to reassessment.

20.8 LEARNING BY EXPERIENCE

Even if the buyer does not end up having to dispose of the target or buy in new management, inevitably some matters will have been missed or poorly judged and some of the activities involved in buying a business will have been conducted inefficiently. Management must learn from their experience if such shortcomings are to be avoided in future and if they are to benefit from apparently wasted costs. Even successful buyers must learn from their experience because they will be expected to be even more successful in the future.

It is inadvisable to leave this learning by experience to informal procedures alone. Memories are short, personnel change and people may cover up or over-react to mistakes. In order to reinforce the learning process, some formal review procedures should be instituted. It is wise to structure this review by reference to the issues identified in our Issues Management Guide to see which were handled well and which not so well. This applies not just to completed but also to aborted acquisitions. All aborted acquisitions will have cost time and money and they may represent opportunities which have been missed as well as disasters which have been avoided.

It is important that management monitor the effective use of the resources, both internal and external, that they commit to searching for and looking at businesses. Those resources are not being used effectively if it takes too long to determine that an acquisition is without prospect of success or if people are too ready to pull out of the process of buying a business because they are over-cautious and too aware of the costs of unsuccessful acquisitions.

Ultimately, buying a business is not an activity for the dilletante. Acquisition is a risky course of action which management should only pursue in a professional manner, on the basis of sound advice and in the firm belief that it is essential to realising their potential.

APPENDIX I

ISSUES MANAGEMENT GUIDE

I.1 ACQUISITION TYPE MATRIX

The following classification of acquisitions is developed in Chapter 3.

	Quality of target's past management		
Strength of target's strategic position	Good	Poor but potential reflected in price	Poor and potential not reflected in price
Poor	No deal	No deal	Asset strip
Good but reflected in price	No deal	No deal	Turn round
Good and not reflected in price	Investment	Turn round	Turn round
Scope for synergy reflected in price	No deal	No deal	Takeover
Scope for synergy not reflected in price	Merger	Takeover	Takeover

Having identified the sort of acquisition which you are pursuing, make sure that you deal with the issues set out in the next section to make the acquisition a success.

I.2 ISSUES BY ACQUISITION TYPE

We return to 12 main issues during the stages of strategy, search, buying and the aftermath. The table below summarises these issues and the types of acquisition to which they are particularly relevant.

	Type of acquisition				
	Asset strip	Turn round	Investment	Takeover	Merger
Target industry knowledge - do you have enough of it?	x	x	x	x	x
Target assessment - can you assess the performance of past management?	x	x	x	x	x
Corrective skills - could you take control of a target and sort it out?		x		x	
Integration skills - could you harmonise two businesses?				x	x
Own industry knowledge - do you understand your own industry's future?				x	x
Competition law - could it prevent your acquisitions?				x	x
Liquidity and dividends - could they be impaired?	x	x	x	x	x
Corporate image - can it withstand your acquisition plans?	x	x		x	x
Job satisfaction - can it be maintained at an acceptable cost?				x	x
Skeletons - might these catch you unawares?	x	x	x	x	x
Stalemate - can this be avoided?	x	x	x	x	x
Strategic purpose - is it achieved by your acquisition plans?	x	x	x	x	x

I.3 STRATEGIC ISSUES

The three main ways of dealing with issues during the strategy phase are identified in Chapter 4.

	Research the issue	Buy in the skills	Alter the strategy
Target industry knowledge	x	x	x
Target assessment	x	x	x
Corrective skills		x	x
Integration skills		x	x
Own industry knowledge	x	x	x
Competition law	x	x	x
Liquidity and dividends			x
Corporate image			x
Job satisfaction			x

I.4 SEARCH ISSUES

The principal techniques for addressing issues during the search phase are described in greater detail in Chapter 6.

	Define an acquisition profile	Meet the key people	Draw up an outline agreement	Prepare a financial appraisal
Target assessment		x		
Corrective skills		x		
Integration skills		x		
Liquidity and dividends				x
Skeletons		x	x	
Stalemate		x	x	x
Strategic purpose	x			x

I.5 BUYING ISSUES

Chapters 7 to 18 explain in detail the way the various activities of the buying process should be conducted to manage the issues effectively. The matrix below gives an overview of how the picture fits together. The scope for seeking legal protection or investigating will be limited when the target is a quoted company. If neither the buyer nor the target is quoted, then the protection of public investors will not be an area for attention. Finally, when assets and not shares are to be bought, the need and scope for legal protection and investigation will be reduced.

	Negotiate	Value	Structure	Legal protection	Investigate	Protect investors
Target industry knowledge		x		x	x	
Target assessment		x		x	x	
Corrective skills		x				
Integration skills		x				
Own industry knowledge		x				
Competition law				x		
Liquidity and dividends		x	x		x	
Corporate image		x			x	x
Job satisfaction		x			x	
Skeletons		x		x	x	
Stalemate	x		x			x
Strategic purpose	x	x			x	

I.6 ISSUES FOR THE AFTERMATH

The post-acquisition initiatives discussed in Chapter 20 and the issues they are intended to deal with are summarised in our final table.

	Communicate and motivate	Manage change positively	Monitor	Buy in skills
Target industry knowledge			x	x
Target assessment			x	x
Corrective skills		x	x	x
Integration skills		x	x	x
Own industry knowledge			x	x
Liquidity and dividends			x	
Corporate image	x	x	x	
Job satisfaction	x	x	x	
Skeletons			x	
Strategic purpose	x	x	x	x

APPENDIX II

AREAS TO INVESTIGATE BEFORE BUYING

II.1 TARGET BACKGROUND

A. Principal locations

Describe sales, manufacturing, administrative and other locations.

B. Ownership

Name the principal shareholders giving the percentages owned by them. In the case of a quoted company also analyse the shareholders by type of investor and size of holding. Where the target is a group, document the group structure.

C. Directors

Name the directors and give details of their age, experience and other affiliations.

D. Professional advisers

Name the principal advisers, such as solicitors, auditors, bankers and stockbrokers and describe the nature and length of their relationships with the company.

E. Brief description of the business

Include all significant business units, their organisational structure, products and services.

F. Brief history of the company

Include any recent significant changes in ownership and business operations.

G. Selling objectives of the company and related information

1. Why is the company for sale?
2. Who are the individuals responsible for the sale of the company?
3. Are there any minority or dissenting shareholders who may affect the sale transaction?
4. What are the proposed terms and conditions of the acquisition including the size and form of the consideration?
5. Is there an anticipated timetable to complete the purchase?
6. What are the tax objectives of the seller?
7. What will be the likely tax consequences for the seller of the proposed transaction?

H. Management

1. What is the reputation of the directors and management?
2. Will they continue after the sale with or without service contracts?
3. Have the company's officers, directors or major shareholders been involved in criminal or other legal proceedings?
4. Have any obvious management actions been taken to make the company look more attractive, for example, by delaying or deferring the costs of bonus schemes, research and development activities, advertising campaigns and maintenance programmes?
5. Is the management of the company affected by any unusual provisions in the memorandum and articles of association?

I. Developments and trends

Describe any recent major developments or trends within the company or the industry.

J. Plans for the future

Obtain recent years' directors' minutes and any marketing studies, operating plans, forecasts and budgets that are available.

K. Related parties

Are the operations of the company significantly impacted by related party transactions? If so, list the parties and describe the relationship and transactions.

L. Major pending or potential litigation

Investigate any such litigation and consider obtaining letters from solicitors assessing the likely outcome.

M. Government regulation

Describe the impact on the business of government restrictions and regulations, for example concerning product, public and employee safety, and identify any licences and approvals which the business has which may not be automatically renewed after an acquisition.

N. Cyclical factors

Describe any seasonal or cyclical factors affecting the company and its industry.

O. Credit and stock market rating

Obtain credit reports and, in the case of a public company, the reports of stockbrokers and investment analysts.

P. Major external forces affecting the company

Describe and note such factors as political uncertainties, industrial disputes and currency movements.

Q. Patents, trademarks and copyrights

Where patents, trademarks and copyrights are important in the company's line of business, describe the major items, indicating any expiration dates and discussing any recent litigation.

II.2 INDUSTRY ANALYSIS

A. Industry structure

1.   Analyse the number of companies by size category and market segment.
2.   Measure the degree of industry concentration.
3.   Summarise recent acquisition trends.
4.   Document recent failures and successes.
5.   Describe the industry in terms of –
     - Geographic location
     - Product lines
     - Channels of distribution
     - Pricing policies
     - Degree of integration
     - Type of customer.
6.   Note any significant barriers facing companies who wish to enter the industry by organic growth, collaboration or acquisition.

B. Industry growth

1.   What are the estimated annual growth rates of sales and profits over recent years?
2.   What are the projected annual growth rates of sales and profits in the foreseeable future?
3.   Describe the principal factors affecting future growth, considering the following possibilities -
     - Demographic trends
     - General economic trends
     - Disposable income trends
     - Sensitivity to interest rate fluctuations
     - Industry composition and trends
     - Market size
     - Technological innovation
     - Product design
     - Economies of scale
     - Product pricing and differentiation
     - Imports and exports
     - Advertising and marketing developments
     - Government regulation
     - Customer buying power
     - Environmental considerations

C. Competition

1. Identify major or similar companies in the industry and ascertain their strategy.
2. Note the nature of any competition from other industries in the form of substitute products.
3. Describe the nature and extent of trade practices and co-operation.
4. In the current competitive environment, identify the key factors for success and the major threats of failure.

D. Customers and suppliers

1. What are the major industries to and from which products are bought and sold and what are their trends in terms of growth and profitability?
2. Has there been significant growth of new customers and suppliers in the last five years?
3. Has there been a trend towards integration of suppliers or customers?
4. Is there a dependence on a few key customers and suppliers?

E. Labour

1. Is adequate skilled labour available and is there a formal system of employee development and training?
2. Are the company's remuneration packages sufficiently competitive to attract suitably qualified and motivated employees?
3. What is the extent of unionisation in the company and the industry?
4. Has the company or industry historically been exposed to industrial relations difficulties?

II.3 ACCOUNTING PROCEDURES AND CONTROLS

A. Accounting policies

1. Obtain a summary of significant accounting policies.
2. Review the auditors' reports and management representation letters for the recent years and identify any issues giving rise to concern or even qualification.
3. Describe any significant recent changes in accounting principles, policies or estimates.

4. Describe any accounting policies that are unique to the company's industry.
5. Describe any accounting policies that differ from industry practice, represent alternative methods where other preferable methods exist, or are excessively conservative or aggressive.
6. Determine if the interim or monthly accounts are prepared on a basis consistent with that of the annual accounts, describing any differences.
7. Describe and assess the impact of major differences from the accounting policies of the buyer.

B. Reporting structure

1. Describe how business units, branches and departments are linked to the central accounting function.
2. Describe in broad outline how the financial and management reporting systems work.

C. Computer facilities

1. List all the company's present computer facilities, noting the location, age and type of each machine and the applications which it runs.
2. List outside computer services used by the company and the applications for which they are utilised.
3. How do users perceive the EDP function and how effective is communication between EDP and user personnel?
4. Document management's current views on how the EDP function is equipped to cope with current and future processing demands and user expectations.

D. Internal controls

1. Describe the processes and objectives of long-range planning and budgetary control, noting the personnel responsible.
    - Do the individuals within the organisation help develop the objectives and plans for their area of accountability, and are plans communicated to the appropriate personnel?
    - Does the budgeting system regularly monitor the accuracy of profit and cash flow forecasts?
    - Are there procedures established to explain major variations between actual and budgeted results on a current basis?
    - Does the company develop and maintain contingency plans in the event of actual results varying significantly from budget?

- How is the profitability of individual business units and product lines monitored?
- Are financial ratios, controllable expense analyses, contribution to overhead analyses, direct costing and other financial evaluation techniques employed?
- What are the principal authorisation limits at different levels for purchasing, investment, recruitment, wage settlements and customer negotiations?

2. Obtain the policies and procedures manual, if any, and broadly assess its comprehensiveness.
3. Determine how compliance with policies and procedures is enforced.
4. Review the external auditors' recent management letters.
5. Where there is an internal audit department, review their recent reports.
6. Based upon the information obtained and further reviews of accounting systems and discussions with management, describe and broadly assess the overall internal control environment, noting any significant weaknesses.

E. Management reports

1. Ascertain whether performance reports are prepared for all major areas of accountability.
2. Evaluate the quality of explanations given for differences between actual and budgeted performance.
3. Obtain copies of key reports used by senior management to monitor and control the business and assess their adequacy for these purposes.
4. For each key report, identify preparers, users, contents, purpose and promptness and frequency of issue and formal procedures for using the report to instigate action and carry out subsequent follow-up.

F. Insurance

1. List property, product liability, key man and other insurance policies, describing significant conditions, benefits and the frequency of review.
2. Identify any unusual policies which indicate types of risk which are specific to the target business.
3. Summarise significant claims filed in recent years.
4. Compare cover to estimated replacement cost of assets held and contingent liabilities.

5.   Establish whether there are any significant unaccrued costs on open or unreported claims.
6.   Ascertain whether increased premiums are anticipated as a result of unfavourable trends or the need for increased coverage.
7.   Enquire whether significant retrospective premium adjustments are anticipated.
8.   Describe the use of other tools of risk management such as forward contracts and options.

II.4 FINANCIAL INFORMATION

A. Balance sheets

Tabulate recent balance sheets for up to 5 years.

B. Assets

1.   Cash
     • Give the name and number of major disbursement accounts.
     • Summarise monthly cash balances for the past year.
     • Identify any restrictions on the use of funds.
     • Specify cash balances denominated in other than local currency.
2.   Debtors
     • Describe the recognition policy for recording sales.
     • List all major debtors, segregating amounts due from customers, employees and others.
     • Identify balances overdue and individual accounts over specified amounts.
     • Describe credit, discount and returns policies and their enforcement.
     • Identify debtors that are discounted or factored, together with the costs, terms and purpose of such arrangements.
     • Describe the company's bad debt reserve policy.
     • Summarise the company's bad debt experience over recent years and the effects of any mitigating measures taken in the form of insurance and retention of title clauses.
     • Obtain support for and determine the reasonableness of general and specific bad debt reserves.
     • Summarise the company's reserve for returns and allowances over recent years discussing any unusual trends and variations with management.
     • Review analyses of debtor ageing and turnover over recent years.

3. Stocks
    - For each major location or product group, analyse stock-holdings, both in terms of raw materials, work-in-progress and finished goods and in terms of material, labour and overhead content.
    - For the different categories of stocks, identify and comment on fluctuations between periods and turnover rates to ensure that these can be explained by business facts rather than accounting inconsistencies.
    - Describe the stock accounting procedures, identifying, for example, whether the company relies on perpetual inventory records, periodic stockcounts or the gross profit method to determine stocks on hand.
    - Describe physical stockcount and cutoff procedures and summarise book-to-physical adjustments at recent counts.
    - Describe the stock reserve policies for excess, slow-moving and obsolete items and the procedures followed to identify such stocks.
    - Describe procedures used to determine net realisable value and to account for problem stocks.
    - Analyse stock reserves and write-downs over recent years and at the last balance sheet date.
    - Comment on seasonal inventory requirements.
    - Describe the stock costing system, noting, for example, the use of job or process costing.
    - Identify the overheads which are included in stock values, the basis for allocating such costs and the recovery rates for recent years and the most recent period.
    - Identify assumptions made about capacity utilisation for purposes of recovering overhead costs and assess their prudence.
    - Determine what methods are used to cost returns, overruns and scrap.
    - Where a full standard costing system is used, obtain explanations of significant variances by product group or cost type for recent years.
4. Investments
    Describe all holdings showing date acquired, percentage held, effective yield, original cost, carrying value and, where relevant, market value.
5. Tangible fixed assets
    - For each major location obtain an analysis by asset category of original cost or subsequent valuation and accumulated depreciation.
    - Document the depreciation rates used for each asset category and compare these to industry norms.

- Assess the possible inappropriateness of depreciation rates by ascertaining the extent of fully written down assets still in use or significant losses arising on fixed asset disposals.
- Identify the means, if any, by which the company substantiates fixed asset balances, for example by using a fixed asset register as a means of conducting fixed asset inventories.
- For all valuations reflected in the accounts, describe the methods of valuation used, the dates of valuation and the qualifications of those performing such valuations.
- Describe any charges over fixed assets.
- Obtain a list of any significant recent fixed asset additions and any major projects currently under construction or contracted.
- Obtain a summary of all significant leasehold improvements, including original cost, accumulated amortisation, the period of amortisation and the related lease expiration dates.
- Describe the company's accounting policies for capitalising installation, construction and interest costs and for recording maintenance expenditure.
- Outline management's plans for fixed asset investment over the foreseeable future and identify any commitments that have been made.
- Analyse management's plans to determine if future capital investment is merely to maintain present capacity or to increase production capabilities in terms of volumes and efficiency.

6. Intangible assets
- Analyse intangible assets between goodwill, brands, deferred expenditure, research and development costs, patents, trademarks and copyrights.
- For each significant item, ascertain its nature and source, describe the company's capitalisation and amortisation policies and identify any limitations on use, liens, threats of loss of value or signs of appreciation.
- Ascertain or estimate the market value of intangible assets not shown in the accounts such as patents, trademarks or copyrights.

C. Liabilities

1. Creditors
- List balances due to major suppliers who constitute more than a specified percentage of trade creditors or total purchases, identifying the nature of the product or service supplied.
- Describe any unusual features of the relationships that exist with the companies listed such as volume discounts, extended terms or long-term commitments.

- Describe normal credit terms and the extent and cost-effectiveness of discounts taken by the company.
2. Accruals
   - Obtain analyses of the current balance and the balance at the previous year-end. Explain significant variations.
   - Ensure that all the required items have been properly accrued, for example, professional fees, employee benefits, payroll and related taxes, holiday pay, claims, probable legal or other contingencies, redundancy and retirement benefits, warranty costs, pension liabilities, planned relocation or shutdown costs, utility charges and goods received but not invoiced.
3. Loans
   - List all banks with whom the company maintains a borrowing relationship and note the total facility available, the current unused portion, the nature of the lender's security, the interest rate, the repayment terms, other conditions, and the facility's review date.
   - Summarise loan agreements and their principal terms.
   - Obtain an analysis of short-term borrowing patterns for recent years noting minimum, maximum and average levels and relating these to the cyclical nature of sales, inventory and production levels and the incidence of fixed asset expenditure.
   - Assess the adequacy of the current facilities to accommodate foreseeable trading levels and capital expenditure plans.
   - Describe any "off balance sheet" financing and summarise the related terms and restrictions.

D. Shareholders' funds

1. Summarise authorised and issued share capital by type.
2. Identify all options to subscribe for shares and any outstanding rights to convert debt into share capital.
3. Document details of share incentive schemes and profit-sharing arrangements.
4. Obtain a shareholders' list.
5. Analyse the origin of the company's reserves and determine the correctness of their classification as distributable and non-distributable.

E. Contingent liabilities and commitments

1. Leases
   - List all leases to which the company is committed, separately identifying both finance leases and operating leases. (A finance

lease transfers substantially all the risks and rewards of ownership associated with a leased asset to the lessee and is generally
evidenced by the lessee being committed to make lease payments which equate to the fair value of the leased asset. Operating leases are leases other than finance leases. Both types of
lease can relate to most types of fixed asset.)
- List future minimum payments under finance leases year by
  year.
- Determine whether such liabilities for future lease payments,
  together with the related leased assets, have been reflected in
  the accounts.
- Determine whether the availability and cost of entering into
  new lease agreements has been assessed.
2. Litigation
- Has the company been involved in any significant litigation in
  the past, or is it threatened by pending or unsettled claims? If
  so, list and describe the nature of those claims and their current
  status, attaching any available legal opinions or representation
  letters provided to the company's auditors.
- Are there any legal problems or potential litigation presently
  facing the industry, for example, regarding employee health,
  product safety, patent infringement and anti-competitive practices? If so, what effect might this have on the company?
3. Other matters
- List any loans for which the company is a guarantor, and assess
  the financial condition of the related companies.
- List all open contracts. Describe the nature and potential cost
  of these contracts including any onerous terms.

F. Profit and loss accounts

Tabulate recent profit and loss accounts for up to five years and, if available, a forecast or budget for the current year and any future years.

G. Profit and loss account analysis

1. Explain fluctuations and trends in sales and gross margin.
2. Identify the company's break-even volume of business and relate
   this to current prospects.
3. Explain changes in overhead expenditure, for example in terms of
   inflation or elements which are related to sales, and identify any
   apparent scope for savings.
4. Rationalise interest income and charges in relation to average rates
   of interest and average balances outstanding during the year.

5. Rationalise the difference between the taxation charge shown in the accounts and the taxation charge indicated by applying the current rate of tax to the profit before tax shown in accounts. The rationalisation would reflect, for example, expenditure not allowed for tax purposes, timing differences not provided for through deferred tax and the benefits of small companies' relief.

6. Identify and quantify any of the following factors which might make previous profit and loss accounts a poor guide for the future performance of the company.
    * Changes required to conform to the buyer's accounting policies.
    * Changes required to conform to anticipated developments in generally accepted accounting principles.
    * Anticipated benefits of post-acquisition synergy.
    * Excessive expenses incurred to reduce taxable profits.
    * Functions performed by or for related parties for which no cost or income has been recorded.
    * Expected changes in raw material costs and overheads.
    * Desired changes in rates of remuneration to ensure that these remain competitive.
    * Adjustments to depreciation charges to reflect revised assessments of the current values or the remaining useful lives of fixed assets.
    * Different bases of providing for deferred taxation.

H. Funds statements

Tabulate recent statements of source and application of funds for up to five years and, if available, a forecast or projection of the cash or funds flow in the current and any future years.

I. Funds statement analysis

1. Review for unusual features or changes between years which would indicate window-dressing or inconsistent cut-off or other accounting procedures between years.

2. Summarise an understanding of how the company has financed its operations in the past and evaluate the feasibility of financing future plans in the same way.

3. Perform a review for a mismatch of sources and applications of funds. For example, an unprofitable company may have been financing fixed asset investment through overdrafts or other short-term loans, thereby exposing itself to future liquidity problems.

J. Use of key ratios

1. Calculate the following key ratios for recent and budgeted periods.

• Return on equity	$= \dfrac{\text{Net profit}}{\text{Shareholders' funds}}$
• Price earnings ratio	$= \dfrac{\text{Share price}}{\text{Earnings per share}}$
• Current ratio	$= \dfrac{\text{Current assets}}{\text{Current liabilities}}$
• Quick ratio	$= \dfrac{\text{Current assets - stock}}{\text{Current liabilities}}$
• Debt to equity ratio	$= \dfrac{\text{Borrowings}}{\text{Shareholders' funds}}$
• Interest cover	$= \dfrac{\text{Profit before interest}}{\text{Interest costs}}$
• Stock turnover	$= \dfrac{\text{Annual cost of sales}}{\text{Average stock}}$
• Debtor turnover	$= \dfrac{\text{Annual credit sales}}{\text{Average debtors}}$

2. Comment on trends in the target's key ratios and compare the ratios to those of the target's competitors and the buyer.
3. Use the results of ratio and other analysis to assess likely and possible future performance and the impact of a potential acquisition on the buyer.

II.5 PERSONNEL

A. General

Obtain a listing of all employees showing their rates of pay, hours of work, job title and length of service.

B. Organisation

1. Obtain the most recent chart or draw up a chart, indicating the number of people employed in each department or location.
2. Are up-to-date job descriptions maintained which define reporting relationships, responsibilities, authorities and bases for performance measurement?

3. Is the organisation structure consistent with current and longer term business requirements?
4. Could savings apparently be made through reorganisation?
5. Are the company's principal personnel policies mutually consistent?
6. Tabulate details of key management meetings including title, function, frequency, membership and achievements.

C. Key personnel

1. Identify key personnel giving position, salary, committed future salary increments, age, health, normal retirement age, experience, skills, qualifications, period of notice and service contract details.
2. What family relationships, if any, exist amongst senior management?
3. Are successful and proven management personnel available to carry out plans?
4. What happens if key employees are not available for an extended period?
5. Are there cohesive lines of authority and communication which facilitate an orderly approach to identifying and tackling problems?
6. Is there excessive domination of operations and planning by any one individual?
7. Have development and training plans been established for key managers and employees with high potential?
8. Does the company have any perceived skill shortages in meeting future plans?
9. What is the strategy for filling key positions?
10. Can internal development and training alone meet future requirements for key personnel or is outside recruiting required?

D. Employee benefits

1. Is the compensation package such as to attract and retain top-quality personnel?
2. Describe the company's pension scheme and, in the case of a defined-benefit scheme, the amount of any underfunding or overfunding.
3. Describe profit-sharing, bonus, share and incentive schemes.
4. Describe holiday policies.
5. Determine if either the buyer or seller would need to upgrade its benefits or salaries as a result of an acquisition.

E. Labour relations

1. Are laws relating to the fair recruitment, training and promotion of women, ethnic minorities and the disabled complied with?
2. Calculate rates of employee turnover in recent years and compare with similar companies and the rates experienced by the potential buyer.
3. Identify all unions with recognised negotiating rights.
4. Identify the numbers and types of employees covered by each union.
5. Determine the renewal date for current pay arrangements and the status of negotiations.
6. Document all industrial disputes occurring in recent years, noting the nature and duration of the action, the unions involved, the cause, the terms of settlement and the impact on the business.
7. Note any labour problems currently anticipated in relation to pay levels and benefits, working practices or proposed redundancies.

II.6 SALES AND MARKETING

A. Product groups

1. Identify all major product and service groups and obtain copies of the company's own advertisements and promotional and technical literature on these products and services.
2. Identify any significant gaps in the range of products and services provided by the company.
3. For each major product and service group provide the following information.
    - Prior year, year-to-date and current year estimated sales and gross margin
    - Orders on hand
    - Date of introduction and maturity of product
    - Major competing products
    - Key components and raw materials
    - Cost, price and discount structure
    - Bases used for costing and pricing
    - Quality and returns history
    - Typical delivery and invoice quantity
    - Customer service and delivery performance
    - Seasonality of demand
    - Market size and share
    - Warranty terms

- Patent and trademark protection
- Technological sensitivity
- Annual production capability.
4. For each major product and service group provide the following customer information.
   - Percentage of sales by major customer for the prior year, year-to-date and estimated current year
   - Percentage of sales by industry use
   - Key selling points in the eyes of customers
   - Means used to promote key selling points

B. Sales and marketing approach

1. How are strategies formulated and modified?
2. How are responsibilities assigned to monitor the implementation and effectiveness of strategies?
3. What are the key sales reports and sources of external information used in monitoring effectiveness?
4. Tabulate levels of advertising expenditure over recent years and relate these to the value of sales, distinguishing between the different media used, point of sale advertising, sponsorship and other forms of promotion.
5. How do advertising expenditures and results compare to those of competitors and firms in similar industries?
6. Who is responsible for the company's other public relations efforts, for example, those aimed at shareholders, lenders, local communities, the workforce and the government?
7. Does the company use an advertising agency or other public relations consultants and, if so, how are the results evaluated?

C. Sales and marketing personnel

1. Relate the company's sales and marketing strategies to the organisation structure.
2. Are employees aware of the company's sales and marketing objectives?
3. Identify key personnel and their experience, age and training.
4. Describe how marketing and sales personnel are motivated, for example through salary, commission and incentive plans.
5. Describe current training programmes.

II.7 PURCHASING

A. Suppliers and subcontractors

1. List the basic raw materials used in the manufacturing process.
2. List all major materials suppliers and subcontractors, noting previous year, year-to-date and current year estimated purchases and any special terms of supply.
3. Determine, principally through discussion with management, the economic condition of the major suppliers' and subcontractors' industries, including competitive structure, and the related possibility of significant raw material shortages, interruption of deliveries or price fluctuations.
4. List and describe any long-term supply contracts and reciprocal buying agreements.
5. Summarise significant purchases from related parties, noting their importance to the company and any special terms involved.

B. Purchasing procedures

1. Obtain a copy of the company's purchasing procedures, or, if not available, document through discussion with management the informal procedures that exist.
2. Highlight any obvious weaknesses which could give rise to non-competitive terms, uneconomic order quantities, obsolescence, overstocking, poor quality, poor service, unauthorised expenditure or "kickbacks".

C. Purchasing organisation

1. Obtain an organisation chart and relate this to the company's purchasing procedures.
2. Identify key personnel and their experience, salary, age and training.

II.8 MANUFACTURING AND DISTRIBUTION

A. Manufacturing and distribution premises

1. Identify each major location.
2. For each major location, identify the information specified below.

- Use
- Dates of construction and acquisition
- Freehold or leasehold
- Cost, book value and estimated current value
- Estimated remaining life
- For short leasehold premises, the current annual rental and the rent review period
- Number of floors and total floor area
- Number of employees
- Present condition
- Capacity utilisation.

B. Machinery and equipment

1. List the principal items of machinery and equipment by location.
2. For the principal items identify the following facts.
   - Age
   - Cost
   - Accumulated depreciation
   - Depreciation rates
   - Condition
   - Replacement cost
   - Production use, specific or general
   - Capacity utilisation.

C. Manufacturing processes

1. Obtain descriptions of the manufacturing processes that take place at each of the major locations.
2. Evaluate each manufacturing process in the terms set out below.
   - Mass production or job shop oriented?
   - Product or process structured flow?
   - Production to order or for stock?
3. Characterise each major manufacturing process in the following respects.
   - The main operations and their sequence, for example, component fabrication and machining, component assembly, final assembly and testing.
   - The relationship of the cost of each operation to the total product cost.
   - The percentage of total factory floor space used for each major operation.
   - The degree of mechanisation and automation for each major operation.

4. Identify the extent to which finished products and components are standardised.
5. What programmes exist for increasing standardisation, ensuring quality control and encouraging employee participation in these programmes?
6. Analyse the total production cycle time in terms of raw material lead time, production engineering lead time and manufacturing time.
7. Document the extent to which subcontractors are used.
8. What are the current trends in manufacturing productivity and how do productivity levels compare to those of competitors?
9. Ascertain whether the company uses any of the following techniques to operate efficiently in the manufacturing and stock management areas.
    * Control of stocks using "ABC", "zero inventory" or "just in time" techniques
    * Set-up and production line time reduction studies
    * Plant utilisation and layout studies
    * Obsolescence reviews
    * Long-term supplier contracts
    * Responsibility accounting for inventory and scrap
    * Value engineering which means involving purchasing personnel in decisions made by engineering regarding the components used in new products
    * Parts standardisation
    * Establishment of a cycle counting programme
    * Reduction of ECN's (engineering change notices)
    * Establishment of a routing system
    * Time and motion studies
    * Make or buy analyses.

D. Maintenance

1. Describe policies on whether to capitalise or write off expenditure.
2. Compare budgeted and actual maintenance and repair expenses for recent years and forecast the expense for the next year, explaining apparent inconsistencies.
3. Describe the company's programme for maintenance and repairs and summarise the internal maintenance facilities.
4. Determine if the company is following its regular maintenance programme and highlight any deferral of preventive maintenance to increase current earnings at the expense of future earnings.

E. Distribution

1. Describe the physical storage and transportation methods in relation to purchases, internal transfers and sales.
2. Estimate the costs involved and relate these to industry norms.
3. Ascertain the scope and findings of any recent studies to compare the costs of using in-house or third party carriers.

II.9 RESEARCH AND DEVELOPMENT

A. Major projects

1. For major projects completed in the last five years, document the nature of the project, the estimated original cost, the final cost, the reasons for major overspends and the estimated benefits.
2. For major projects currently in progress, document the nature of the project, costs to date, estimated time and cost to complete and the anticipated benefits.
3. For future major projects, document whether the project has been approved and what the purpose, expected timescale and estimated costs of the project are.
4. Describe any significant projects currently being undertaken or recently completed by competitors.
5. Identify how the company's current research and development programme aims to develop new or improved products to satisfy current customers' needs and customer needs presently being met by other products or competitors.
6. Document how research and development needs are identified, assessed, acted upon and costed.
7. Judge whether the company is able to maintain its present competitive position in the light of recent, current and proposed major projects.

B. Resources

1. Identify research and development personnel, their terms of employment, technical competence, effectiveness and responsibilities.
2. Review the adequacy of current and proposed staffing arrangements to cope with current and proposed major projects.
3. Assess whether the company's current laboratory and other facilities are adequate to satisfy the needs of current and proposed major projects or whether capital investment is required.

II.10 TAXATION

A. Corporation tax

1. Identify tax years still open and estimate the possible underprovision in the accounts based on a review of draft tax computations, where these have not been submitted, or points raised by the Inland Revenue, where computations have been submitted.
2. Ascertain whether interest and penalties may be charged by the Inland Revenue on tax years not yet agreed.
3. Review correspondence files between the company's tax agents and the Inland Revenue.
4. Review the conditions of any clearances given by the Inland Revenue in relation to previous reorganisations or demergers affecting the target company.
5. If the company is a close company, answer the following questions.
   - Have apportionment clearances been obtained for all years?
   - Has any tax on loans or benefits-in-kind to participators been properly accounted for?
6. If the company is a member of a group, answer the following questions.
   - If ACT or income tax has not been accounted for on intragroup dividends or interest respectively, is a group income election in force?
   - Have any assets been transferred to the company from another group company during the past six years, so giving rise to a tax liability if the company leaves the group?
   - Has the company entered into depreciatory transactions with other group companies which would have the effect of artificially reducing the value of the company?
   - Have group loss relief claims and surrenders of ACT been agreed by the Inland Revenue after agreeing the tax computations of both parties to such relief for the relevant period?
7. Review recent CT61 forms relating to ACT and income tax.
8. Identify rollover relief claims which might give rise to otherwise unanticipated chargeable gains on disposals of fixed assets.
9. Analyse any unrelieved ACT available for carry forward, identifying any surrendered ACT which would not be available for use after an acquisition.
10. Analyse any trading losses available for carry forward, identifying stock relief losses which may lapse.

B. VAT and import duty

1. Review VAT correspondence files, examining VAT returns submitted and seeing whether control visits have highlighted any serious problems.
2. Ascertain whether the company makes exempt supplies which could give rise to an unrecognised partial exemption problem with VAT having been wrongly reclaimed on certain purchases.
3. Check that liabilities for import VAT and duty under deferment arrangements are properly recorded and that import VAT is only reclaimed when a certificate of payment is held.
4. Review customs correspondence files for outstanding queries regarding the valuation and classification of goods for duty purposes and the operation of quota exemptions or anti-dumping provisions.
5. Document any approvals or authorisations for duty relief or simplified procedures which will involve taking on an obligation or which will require re-negotiation before they are transferred to another company.

C. PAYE and NIC

1. Identify the company's pay practices.
2. Review the company's procedures for complying with PAYE and NIC regulations.
3. Review PAYE correspondence files, examining P35's submitted for previous years together with payments to the collector of taxes and noting whether there has been a recent control visit and if so, what was the result.
4. Confirm that P11D's and P9D's detailing employee benefits have been submitted in respect of those earning more or less than £8,500 per annum, respectively.
5. Where sub-contractors are used, check that appropriate exemption certificates have been examined before making payments gross.
6. Enquire about any other gross payments.

APPENDIX III

OUTLINE WARRANTIES AND INDEMNITIES

III.1 INTRODUCTION

Warranties and indemnities, which are introduced in Chapter 13, exist to address certain of the risks involved in buying a business except where the purchase takes the form of buying shares in a public company. Fewer warranties are required when buying business assets rather than private company shares and no taxation indemnity is required in an asset purchase.

This appendix should help management to appreciate and monitor the important activities of their legal advisers during an acquisition. However, our outline warranties and indemnities may differ in two respects from those which would appear in a real purchase agreement.

1. In a specific acquisition, some of the risks covered in our summary will be irrelevant and some will need to be tackled more comprehensively.
2. The wordings used are colloquial and lack the precision that would be required in a formal legal document.

The differences illustrate the necessity of seeking experienced and qualified legal advice when drafting warranties and indemnities. A final point of contrast may arise because our warranties are organised under headings which broadly follow the structure adopted in this book. An actual schedule of warranties is likely to be ordered differently and may not be divided under headings. Buyers should however encourage their solicitors to organise the warranties under headings which do aid understanding.

III.2 THE RULES OF THE GAME

Before becoming embroiled in the specific information that is to be confirmed by the seller through warranties, it is necessary to establish what sort of information is being provided to the buyer. In this respect, the buyer should seek the warranties set out below.

- All information supplied by the sellers and the target's management, agents and advisers is true in all respects.
- The information supplied is complete and covers all matters which are relevant to a buyer.

The seller will try to qualify such warranties by making reference to "material items" only and by inserting phrases such as "so far as the vendor is aware" or "to the best of the vendor's information, knowledge and belief".

Rules of the game also need to be established, where there is more than one seller, to determine who will be liable for damages awarded for the breach of warranties. The liability of the sellers may be several or joint and several. Where liability is several, sellers will be liable in proportion to their shareholdings in the target company. Where liability is joint and several, an action may be brought against one of the sellers for the full amount of any claim.

Finally, it should be noted that it is usual for a schedule of warranties to be accompanied by a "disclosure letter". In this letter, the seller sets out in more detail any information referred to in the warranties and also documents the nature of all exceptions to the warranties given.

If any arguments develop after an acquisition, much may turn on the language and content of the disclosure letter. Where there has been a full investigation performed on the part of the buyer, the seller may insist that "everything" was disclosed to the investigators and that therefore everything was effectively disclosed for the purpose of the contract. It is therefore important to ensure that the disclosure letter is comprehensive. Buyers should also insist that drafts of the disclosure letter and the supporting documents are produced as early as possible in the negotiations and are subsequently updated on a regular basis. Buyers should avoid having to make snap decisions on the basis of large quantities of information which are delivered late in the day.

III.3 ACCOUNTS

The accounts of the target are of crucial importance in valuing the target business in the way described in Chapter 8. The accounts of the target are also essential in understanding the target's past, present and future operations as we saw in Chapter 15.

Therefore, no matter what work has been performed to verify the accounts by way of the purchase investigation or the acquisition audit referred to in Chapter 14, the buyer will seek warranties on the accounting information supplied by the seller. Consequently, warranties along the lines set out below should be considered for inclusion.

- Complete and accurate accounting records have been maintained and retained in accordance with the requirements of company legislation.
- The statutory accounts relied upon by the buyer have been prepared in accordance with company legislation to give a true and fair view of the target's state of affairs and performance.
- Common accounting policies have been consistently applied between years except where the effects of changes have been noted and quantified.
- All extraordinary and exceptional items have been identified.
- Assets are not stated at amounts in excess of their realisable value.
- Established liabilities are reflected in full.
- Proper provisions and disclosures have been made in respect of contingent, deferred, unquantified or disputed liabilities and commitments.
- The accounts are not distorted by any window-dressing transactions or off balance sheet financing.
- The nature and effect of all transactions with related parties have been disclosed.
- Post balance sheet events have been completely and adequately disclosed and, where relevant, reflected in the statutory accounts by way of adjustment.
- Any management accounts submitted to the buyer have been properly prepared on bases which are consistent with those adopted in preparing the statutory accounts.

III.4 INFORMATION ABOUT PROSPECTS

The buyer's assessment of post-acquisition prospects discussed in Chapter 15 is not based on the target's accounts alone. The buyer will also rely on industry studies obtained from sources other than the seller and on the buyer's own experience. In these circumstances warranties are clearly inappropriate.

However, the buyer will seek assurances on major areas of risk such as employment liabilities, legal problems and tax skeletons to which we shall shortly refer in more detail. Before that, we will list some of the other information relating to future operations on which warranties will be sought.

• Current bank facilities are fully disclosed and are adequate to ensure that the target has sufficient working capital to continue to transact its present level of business.

• Terms of trade in relation to debtors and creditors have not been changed or dishonoured since the date of the last accounts and will not be changed or dishonoured in the foreseeable future.

• Since the last accounts date, there has been no deterioration or significant change in the target's activities, level of trading, profitability or prospects.

• The quantities of stocks held by the target are both marketable and adequate but not excessive.

• The buildings of the target are in a good state of repair, fit for their present purposes, free from structural problems or compulsory purchase orders and properly served by rights of access and public utilities.

• The plant, machinery and other equipment of the target have been properly maintained and are in a good and safe state of repair and working order.

• The target and its assets are adequately covered against fire, accident, damage, injury, third party loss, loss of profits and other risks and nothing has been done to make such insurance void or subject to increased premiums.

• No insurance claims are outstanding by or against the target.

• There are no outstanding commitments relating to the purchase or sale of capital assets.

III.5 EMPLOYMENT LIABILITIES

As discussed in Chapter 16, it is important for a buyer to establish the extent of obligations to the target's employees whether in a share or asset purchase.

• Full particulars have been disclosed about all employees, including name, age, length of service, terms and conditions of employment, profit-sharing and bonus arrangements and long-term service agreements.

• The last alterations of salaries and other terms of employment prior to completion of the acquisition have been notified to the buyer.

- All trade union recognition agreements have been disclosed and there are no outstanding matters likely to give rise to industrial action.
- No liability has been incurred for breach of an employment contract or service agreement or other action by the target in relation to an employee.

The pitfalls of target company pension schemes were also referred to in Chapter 16 and shown below are warranties which afford some protection against such pitfalls.

- All relevant documents relating to the target's pension scheme have been disclosed, including the trust deed and the latest actuarial report and accounts.
- Full disclosure has been made of the pension scheme's assets, membership, investment policies, contribution rates and scales of benefit.
- The contributions paid to the scheme are sufficient to fund, at a minimum, those benefits earned to date, calculated on the basis of projected salaries at normal retirement dates.
- The scheme has "contracted-out" status which allows the target to calculate its NIC liabilities at reduced rates.

III.6 LEGAL HAZARDS

Chapter 16 was concerned not only with employment liabilities but also with legal hazards relating to outstanding litigation, title disputes, corporate constitution and contractual obligations. Accordingly, warranties should be sought to address these risks.

- The target is not involved in any civil litigation or any arbitration or tribunal proceedings and there are no circumstances likely to give rise to such litigation or proceedings.
- Any claims against the target being pursued by customers, employees or others are adequately covered by insurance.
- The target has conducted its affairs in accordance with all applicable laws and regulations of the countries in which it operates. These laws and regulations would include those relating to corruption, fair trading, restrictive practices, data protection and company registration.
- There is no actual or pending prosecution for any criminal offence committed by the target or by one of its officers, agents or employees carrying out their duties for the target.
- The target has obtained and complied with all the necessary licences, consents and permits which it requires to carry on its business.

- Under the terms of the relevant offer letters, the target is not liable to repay any government grants as a result of either an acquisition or any other action taken before the proposed sale.

- The target has not supplied faulty or defective products or negligent services likely to give rise to future liabilities.

- The target has not entered into any contracts, activities or transactions which are beyond its powers, invalid or otherwise unenforceable.

- The target owns all the assets and has good and marketable title to all the properties, subsidiaries and investments shown in the accounts.

- The target has possession of all assets and title deeds free from encumbrances such as mortgages.

- In respect of intellectual assets, such as know-how or trade secrets, no disclosure has been made to third parties except in accordance with enforceable confidentiality agreements which have been disclosed to the buyer.

- The sellers are entitled to sell and transfer to the buyer full legal and beneficial ownership of the target's shares free from all liens, charges and encumbrances without requiring any third party consent.

- The memoranda and articles of association and statutory books of the target and its subsidiaries have been made available and are accurate, complete and up-to-date in all respects.

- There are no arrangements or agreements in force which grant any person the right to call for the issue, allotment or transfer of any share or loan capital of the target company or any of its subsidiaries.

- All contractual commitments of the target have been disclosed, including those which are onerous, unusual, not at arm's length or liable to be terminated as a result of the acquisition. Such contractual commitments include agreements relating to debt, leasing, hire purchase, franchising, distribution, after sales service and long-term purchases or sales. Any guarantees, mortgages and indemnities are also covered.

- The target is not a member of any unincorporated joint venture, consortium, partnership or other association which exposes it to unlimited liability.

- There is no undisclosed power of attorney or other authority outstanding by which a person may transact business on behalf of the target.

III.7 TAXATION WARRANTIES

Taxation warranties are sought to provide assurance in relation to both the potential tax skeletons which we examined in Chapter 17 and the tax planning exercises which we described in Chapter 11. Some typical taxation warranties are shown below.

*   Subject to specified exceptions, all necessary tax returns have been properly made and agreed with the taxation authorities and the tax has been punctually paid. Warranties should cover corporation tax, ACT, VAT, PAYE, NIC and other taxes, even those no longer in force.
*   Tax trading losses, unrelieved ACT, capital losses and tax written down values are as disclosed and analysed by the seller.
*   The target is not and has never been a close company.
*   For a close company, clearances have been obtained for all relevant years to ensure that the Inland Revenue will not "apportion" any of the target's undistributed profits and tax them as if they were income received by the shareholders. Under this process, if the shareholders declined to pay the tax due on the apportioned income, then the company itself could become liable.
*   For a close company, no deemed distributions in the form of loans or benefits-in-kind have been made to a director or major shareholder.
*   When the target is a member of a group, all assets and liabilities in respect of group loss relief and surrendered ACT shown in the accounts have been agreed with the Inland Revenue.
*   All claims for rollover relief made by the target to defer corporation tax on chargeable gains have been disclosed.
*   All fixed assets acquired by the target from fellow group companies during the past six years have been properly disclosed. This disclosure allows a buyer to identify the chargeable gains which would arise upon buying a target from out of a group.
*   There are no reasons not covered elsewhere why the target would incur a corporation tax liability on the disposal at book value of any asset acquired from the target.
*   There is no likely restriction on the ability of the target to offset past trading losses against future profits as a result of a major change in the nature or conduct of its trade prior to the acquisition or because the trade has become small or negligible.
*   There is no likely restriction on the ability to offset the target's past unrelieved ACT against its future mainstream corporation tax liability.

- No artificial or unusual transactions have been entered into by the target for the purpose of avoiding tax which may lead to the Inland Revenue taking action to ignore their effects.

III.8 THE TAXATION INDEMNITY

The taxation risks to a buyer are usually covered not only by warranties which give remedy through damages but also through a deed of indemnity which allows the buyer to obtain full recompense for any loss incurred.

Under a deed of indemnity the seller of a company will agree to make good any loss suffered by either the buyer or the target company where that loss is attributable to events occurring prior to the date of the deed. The loss can take the form of either a claim for taxation or a denial of relief by the Inland Revenue.

The indemnity can specify all the particular circumstances in which a loss could occur, including those set out in the previous section on taxation warranties. Alternatively, the indemnity can be framed in general terms subject to specific exclusions. The exclusions would relate to tax which was provided for in the accounts or tax which arose as a result of some failure of the buyer or a retrospective increase in tax rates.

Furthermore, sellers will usually seek additional protection in the deed of indemnity by specifying an upper limit to their liability, resisting minimal claims, imposing time restrictions and offsetting over-estimates of other tax liabilities which were reflected in the accounts at the time of the acquisition.

Naturally, the principles involved in framing a deed of indemnity relating to any sufficiently important non-taxation matters, such as returns of defective goods, will be similar to those outlined in the taxation example.

INDEX